FIDDLER ON THE ROOF OF AFRICA

"Should be required reading for people contemplating joining the Peace Corps."
—Ambassador Gregory W. Engle, Peace Corps Country Director

FIDDLER ON THE ROOF OF AFRICA

HOW TO FAIL SUCCESSFULLY AS A PEACE CORPS VOLUNTEER

DEREK LOWSTUTER

SPRING CEDARS

Copyright © 2024 by Derek Lowstuter

All rights reserved

First edition, 2024

Cover and book design by Spring Cedars
Cover photo: Scout in Simien Mountains National Park

ISBN 978-1-963117-33-2 (paperback)
ISBN 978-1-963117-34-9 (hardback)
ISBN 978-1-963117-35-6 (ebook)

Published by Spring Cedars
Denver, Colorado
www.springcedars.com

TABLE OF CONTENTS

GLOSSARY vii

ACKNOWLEDGEMENTS xi

PREFACE: WHAT'S IN A NAME? xiii

PART I 17

    WRECKAGE 19

    BLESS THE RAINS DOWN IN AFRICA 27

    PEACE "CORPSE" 33

    SHIT AND SUGARCANE 41

    THREADING THE NEEDLE(S) 49

    WELCOME TO DEBARK 57

    DEEP ROOTS 67

    THE VIRTUE OF RAPE 75

    PINKIES UP 89

    SMILING WITH DEATH 101

PART II 109

    THE WAR ON VEGAN MONKEYS 111

    ONWARD AND UPWARD 123

    AFRICA AT 15,000 FEET 131

    CLOUDY WITH A CHANCE OF GOATS 141

    SOMETHING WICKED THIS WAY COMES 151

    EROSION 163

PART III 173

    RUNNING DRY 175

ON HOLIDAY	185
STREET DOG	193
THE UGLY ROCK	203
AWFULLY GOOD. TERRIBLY FANTASTIC. PRETTY UGLY.	213
CATHARSIS	225
FINDING SERENITY	231
HOW TO FAIL SUCCESSFULLY	239
EPILOGUE	251
REFERENCES	253
ABOUT THE AUTHOR	263

GLOSSARY

Abbreviations

ADP	Amhara Democratic Party
ANRS	Amhara National Regional State
AS	Administrative Separation
AU	African Union
COS	Close Of Service
ET	Early Termination
EWCA	Ethiopia Wildlife Conservation Authority
FAO	UN Food and Agriculture Organization
FFW	Food For Work
GIZ	German Development Cooperation (in German)
GLOW	Girls Leading Our World
MDG	Millennium Development Goals
MS	Medical Separation
NGO	Non-Governmental Organization
ODP	Oromo Democratic Party
ORS	Oral Rehydration Salts
PCV	Peace Corps Volunteer
RPCV	Returned Peace Corps Volunteer
SEPDM	Southern Ethiopian People's Democratic Movement
SDG	Sustainable Development Goals
SMNP	Simien Mountains National Park
SNNPR	Southern Nations, Nationalities, and Peoples Region
TPLF	Tigray People's Liberation Front
UN	United Nations
UNESCO	UN Educational, Scientific, and Cultural Organization
WWII	World War Two

Amharic Words

Abet	Yeah, what's up?
Abiy	Great, important
Ambasha	A slightly sweet round loaf of bread
Amhareñña	Amharic language
Aye	No
Ayfekadum	Forbidden, not permitted
Berbere	A complex spice mixture used in Ethiopian dishes
Bet	House, building, or collective group of people
Betam	Very
Birtucaan	Orange
Chika bet	Buildings made of mud, straw, and wood poles
Cuchella motaya	The place where puppies die
Dabeñña	Loyal customer or vendor
Debark	Town name derived from the words agreement and prowl
Demera	Celebratory fire
Derek	Stubborn, stiff, dry
Derg	Council
Dinkenesh	Name meaning you are a wonderful woman
Doriye	Thug
Falasha	Ethiopian Jewish
Fano	A guerilla/militia fighting force
Fendisha	Popcorn
Ferenj(i)	Foreigner
Filwuha	Hot springs
Ful	A spicy bean stew
Ezi-bet	Is anyone in?
Gabi	Handwoven white cloth worn over upper body
Ge'ez	Ancient Semitic language

Gesho	Buckthorn leaves
Gobez	Clever
Guramayle	A combination language composed of other languages
Habesha	Ethiopian people
Ishee	OK
Ityopia	Ethiopia
Ityopiawi	Ethiopian
Jebena	Percolating clay pot for brewing coffee
Jibb	Hyena
Kay Kabaro	Red fox, Amharic name for Ethiopian wolf
Kebele	Neighborhood
Kiremt	Rainy season
Kitfo	A spicy dish of minced raw beef
Kolo	Roasted barley snack
Konjo	Beautiful
Kosso	African Redwood tree
Leba	Thief
Lukso	A traditional Ethiopian funeral or wake
Maqwamiya	Prayer staff
Mender	Village
Meskel	Cross
Neyn	I am
Oww	Yes
Samenañña	Dialect composed of mostly Amharic and Tigrayan
Shifta	Bandit
Shiro	A common Ethiopian chickpea soup or stew
Simien	North
T'ella	Traditional Ethiopian beer
Tankara	Strong

Techawot	Telling someone to have fun
Tenadam	Adam's health, Amharic name for rue
Tewahedo	United as one (in Ge'ez)
Tigreñña	Tigrayan language
Tikus	Hot or fresh
Timket	Orthodox Christian celebration of the Ethiopian Epiphany
Wolfram	Fat
Woreda	County/District
Wuha	Water
Yaselam Guad	The body of peace, Amharic name for Peace Corps
Zinab	Rain

A note on Ethiopia naming practices:

Most Ethiopians are given a first name with a literal meaning significant to their parents. For example, the name Abiy means "great" or "important." Ethiopians don't have a surname that is passed down generationally like Western cultures. Instead, their last name is usually the name of their father. This is called a patronym. The Ethiopian prime minister is Abiy Ahmed. His father was Ahmed Ali, so Abiy took Ahmed as his last name. This can be confusing when people from other cultures write or speak about Ethiopians. Calling Abiy "Mr. Ahmed" is understandable but incorrect. To avoid this confusion, it is best to use a full name, such as "Mr. Abiy Ahmed," or the common honorific Ato (Mr.), such as "Ato Abiy." Woizero (Mrs.) and Woizerit (Ms.) are the titles used for married and unmarried women, respectively.

ACKNOWLEDGEMENTS

I would like to express my gratitude to everyone who made this book possible. First and foremost, my heartfelt thanks go to my family for their support, patience, and encouragement throughout not only the writing process, but also during the years I spent in Ethiopia. Care packages have a special kind of magic. I am especially thankful to my wife, Claire, who served with me and encouraged my efforts to somehow communicate that transformative experience.

Thank you to our friends and colleagues in Ethiopia Group 4 (G4), and other groups, whom we trained and served with. I raise a lukewarm bottle of Hakim Stout in your honor. Thank you to the reviewers who collectively labored to help me weave together my feelings and research into a (mostly) coherent whole.

Finally, I would like to acknowledge the countless authors, researchers, and thinkers whose works inspired this project. Without their contributions, this book would not have been possible.

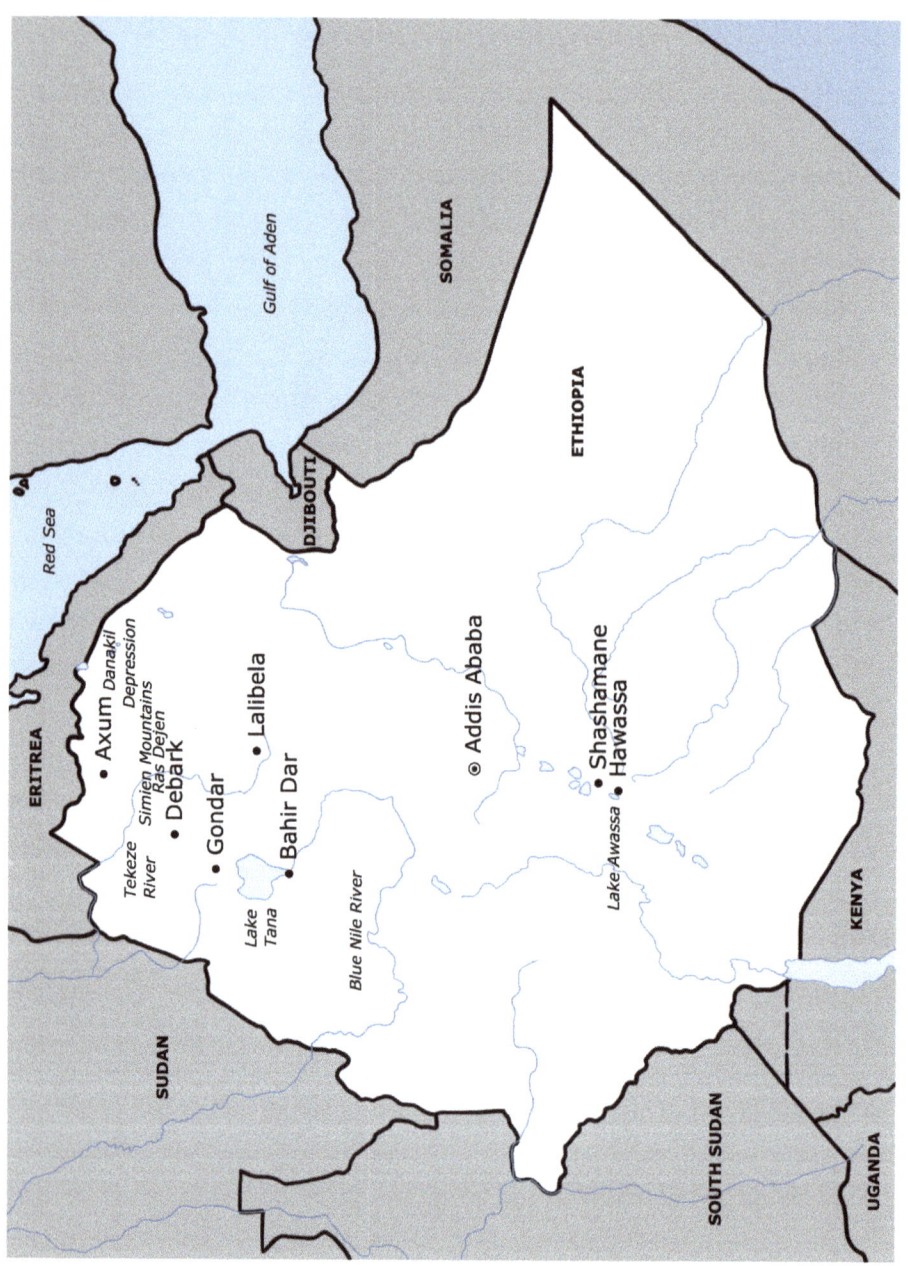

Map of Ethiopia

PREFACE: WHAT'S IN A NAME?

It has been a long time since I saw my high school's production of *Fiddler on the Roof*. Although the opening lines still resonate; "Every one of us is a fiddler on the roof trying to scratch out a pleasant, simple tune without breaking his neck." This captures the reality of living and working in a developing country. Every continent, country, and community is unique, but there are more similarities than differences that connect the lives of people around the world. We are all fiddlers trying to scratch out a pleasant, simple tune without breaking our necks.

As I write this, it has been over a decade since I spent two years working in rural Ethiopia as a Peace Corps Volunteer (PCV), an international program of the United States government. After only a year of marriage, my wife Claire and I were selected to join the first group of conservation Volunteers heading to Ethiopia. Instead of fading, the events we experienced have become more vivid and left a lasting impact on the way we view life in developing countries and at home in the USA.

This book borrows its title and many of its themes from our work with ethnic groups living in and around Simien Mountains National Park (SMNP). The park is a protected natural area in Ethiopia's northern state of Amhara. Its economic, social, and environmental importance for the country cannot be overstated. It was an honor to serve in the Simien Mountains on conservation, education, and health projects.

The Ethiopian highlands represent two distinct mountainous areas in the Horn of Africa. These twin mountain ranges rise on either side of the Great Rift Valley like monolithic waves. The mountains ripple out from the geological violence of the rift itself, where the Earth is literally pulling itself apart. Ethiopia's mountains represent nearly half of all high-elevation areas in tropical Africa—leading Ethiopia to be called "The Roof of Africa." Some other locations, such as Mount Kilimanjaro in neighboring Tanzania, dubiously claim that distinction based on highest elevation alone. After all, it's the Roof of Africa, not the top shingle of Africa. Additionally, SMNP's first modern warden, C.W. Nicol, wrote of his experiences attempting to manage the park during imperial rule in his book *From the Roof of Africa*.

The contention is understandable because one of the lowest points in Africa, and Earth, also lies in Ethiopia. The Danakil Depression in the northeast of Ethiopia is a beautiful hellscape of volcanic sulfur vents and boiling salt water that drops more than 400ft (122m) below sea level. It is one of the hottest and most inhospitable places on Earth, but is also a popular site to explore for foreign visitors. Ethiopia is both roof and foundation.

The highest point in Ethiopia is the summit of Ras Dejen (alternatively spelled Ras Dashen) at roughly 14,930ft (4,550m). The peak is difficult to differentiate from the surrounding landscape of ancient lava flows and is located within the boundaries of SMNP. The exact elevation at the summit is based on opinion as much as geographical fact. Estimates vary by up to 100ft (30m) depending on whom you ask, when they learned the "correct" answer, and how willing they are to accept they are wrong, like many things in Ethiopia.

Ethiopia is a remarkably rich country of unique cultures and ecosystems—powerfully argued by some to be more varied and valuable than any other place on Earth. This book covers only a small fraction of this abundance. Although warranted, criticisms of Ethiopia or unfavorable memories of times spent there should be interpreted as disapproval of a loved one and not bitterness toward Ethiopia or its people. According to American naturalist John Muir, "Going to the mountains is going home." The Ethiopian highlands were, and always will be, a second home and roof over my head.

This book is a mix of academic study and personal observations—equal parts literature review, introspection, scholarly analysis, confabulation, with a pinch of classic ethnocentrism. Peace Corps service is exceptionally context specific and each PCV has experiences and outcomes unique to the time spent working with their host community and partners. Every Volunteer is different and every community is different. The reactions that take place between the two can be unpredictable and chaotic.

The goal of this book is to address broad international development issues that play out around the world, such as food aid, environmental conservation, cultural traditionalism, and development theory. These topics are viewed through the lens of a PCV in Ethiopia. International development conversations are often dry, distant, and lack a personal connection to what is discussed. The richness of personalities and events becomes background noise, or worse, statistics. The chapters of this book ground these topics in first-hand experiences and observations to make them more engaging and accessible. Because of this, the chapters follow themes of international development and trains of thoughts. The chapters are sequential but not always chronological.

So, let's tune our fiddles and start the climb.

PART I

WRECKAGE

"Millions of deaths would not have happened if it weren't for the consumption of alcohol. The same can be said about millions of births."
—Mokokoma Mokhonoana

"We cannot care for everyone. [...] Caring itself is reduced to mere talk about caring when we attempt to do so."
—Nel Noddings

"Ouch..." I exhaled while the reality of the situation hit me in the face as hard as my airbag *should* have. I was back in the USA. My Peace Corps service was over. I was in a wreck. I had regained consciousness only seconds before and was still waiting for body parts to start complaining. Picking my head off the steering wheel, I looked up to see the crumpled hood of my beloved 20-year-old hatchback. The rear bumper of the truck in front of me was casually resting in my car's engine compartment, kissing my windshield wipers. Its driver was already on the phone with 911, pacing between my window and the back of his lifted pickup.

Another man, the driver of the car that rear-ended me and shoved my car under the truck, was crouched by my open driver door. *Did I open the door or did he?* I tried to focus on his face. It took several seconds to realize he was asking if I needed an ambulance. The pickup driver had overheard and was nodding aggressively at him. He was angry—not just at the inconvenience of someone else causing a car accident, but also at the man's appearance. His car was a crusty, old Buick with mismatched body panels and black garbage bags duct-taped where two windows should have been.

The man matched his vehicle. He was probably in his late 20s, but his hair was disheveled, his face tan and mottled by several small patches of scabs. His T-shirt wasn't ripped, rather so threadbare it was translucent in spots. He asked if I was OK, with genuine concern. His teeth glared a surprisingly brilliant white, while the whites of his eyes were anything but.

I winced at the pain in my face and along my shoulder, where the seatbelt had dug into my skin. More worried about my car than myself, I glanced at my hood again and realized my car wouldn't be driving again...ever. I found my phone wedged in the passenger seat and scrolled through my contacts, stopping at a familiar name. *Claire...that's my wife's name, right? Of course it is. That's stupid.* I questioned myself again then decisively pressed the call button. Claire answered quickly, and her cheery response seemed out of place because she obviously didn't know about the wreck.

"I got in an accident, and they are taking me to the hospital to get me checked out. I won't make it to daycare."

"Were you texting?!" she demanded and then abruptly changed her tone, "Are you OK?"

"No, I got rear-ended. I think I'm fine, but I should go to the hospital to make sure."

She jumped into problem-solving mode and said she would ask a friend to pick up our daughter at daycare.

I sank into my seat. The ambulance arrived and the paramedics gingerly scooped me onto the backboard—avoiding my undeployed airbag like a landmine. I was evaluated in the ambulance and asked basic questions to determine if I had any obvious brain damage. My answers were correct, but slow.

"What city are we in?"

How should I know? I'm not the one driving the ambulance.

"Do you understand you were in an accident?"

No shit, I'm in an ambulance.

"Who is the president?"

Some old white guy.

I felt heavy and my limbs weren't as responsive as they should be. *That's OK. I'm just tired. Right?* I was mostly conscious and mostly confused as the ambulance worked its way through traffic. Oddly, I started thinking of another wreck from more than 10 years prior on a completely different continent. I was not in one of the vehicles involved, but I watched the wreck happen in the same detached way I was in when answering the paramedics questions.

The wreck was in Addis Ababa, the sprawling capital city of Ethiopia. Meaning "New Flower" in Amharic, the cosmopolitan city is considered by some to be the capital of all Africa. It is almost 8,000ft (2,400m) above sea level and home to roughly 5.5 million people in 2024. While censuses in Africa are notoriously inaccurate, what was once a resort town for Ethiopian elites has become the country's capital and a city larger than Los Angeles. Addis, as the city is often abbreviated, is the headquarters of numerous international organizations. This includes the African Union (AU) which, like the European Union (EU), attempts to represent member states from around the continent. Ethiopia's relative political and social stability, and its geographical location, have encouraged development agencies from around the world to establish a presence there.

All that activity requires lots of roads, which incomprehensibly lack formal names. Navigation and postal deliveries are accomplished through landmarks and local place names. This makes finding your way in the city difficult if you aren't familiar with any of the reference points. I remember thinking, this city of millions has skyscrapers and an international airport but not addresses?

Most Ethiopians rely on the ubiquitous blue and white minivans for daily trips around the city. These "blue donkeys" ferry people on established routes, with passengers getting on and off as they make the rounds—like a full-sized bus, but much nimbler—perfect for maneuvering through the constant traffic and evading police if needed. One night, I made the mistake of getting on a minibus that was carrying more people than was legal. When told to stop at a police checkpoint, the driver decided to try to outrun the police. A slow but suspenseful chase resulted in the van escaping, but dropping passengers off in an alley blocks away from where I was supposed to be. Many well-to-do Ethiopians and international visitors prefer contract taxis that take them directly to any location they want in the city. However, PCVs cannot afford these taxis on a regular basis and instead share the cramped minivans with the constant flow of men, women, children, and livestock.

It was one of those blue donkeys I thought about while the ambulance I rode in wove through traffic. I was in a group of Volunteers walking back to our hotel in Addis after having dinner at a nearby pizza place when we heard a deafening CRACK behind us. We were in town together for training and our reactions to the racket were slowed by glasses of *tej*, a delicious honey wine. We were walking on the side of the road and had just started to turn when a minibus skidded past us at full speed—on its side. It spun slowly as it flew past us, and the sliding door grating on the road left graceful loops of navy-blue calligrapher's ink on the pavement until the minibus shuddered to a stop against the crude concrete median.

The other Volunteers and I stood stunned at the abrupt

Minibus taxi in Addis. Photo by Ryan Kilpatrick, Flickr.

appearance of the minibus and the even more abrupt silence that followed. A wail erupted from behind us as the once deserted street filled with people coming out from the surrounding dark buildings. Within 30 seconds, a group of Ethiopians had encircled the minibus and were attempting to rock it back upright. The wail we heard had come from a short, middle-aged woman who collapsed on the curb and was now sobbing silently into her hands.

Peace Corps staff repeatedly instructed Volunteers to never get involved in life threatening situations, another's life or ours. There are too many things that can go wrong and too many opportunities for Volunteers or the Peace Corps itself to be blamed. Not thinking, I ran to the vehicle that had hit the minibus. The black SUV had a crumpled engine compartment, and a steady drip of dark fluid had begun to pool underneath. An older Ethiopian man in a beige suit and blood-red power tie was standing next to the open driver side door.

He groggily responded in English when I asked in Amharic if he was OK. "What happened?" he blurted.

"You were in a car accident." I replied in English, guiding him to the median.

I turned to see the minibus balancing on two wheels right before the crowd was able to tip it back on all four. The minibus rocked violently, sounding like a shaken jar of marbles. The driver's head flopped to his left side. If he wasn't killed in the initial impact, the chaotic righting of the minibus likely had. His head rolled back and forth in front of and then behind his shoulder as if his spine took a sharp bend right below his skull.

The minibus accelerator was floored, and the vehicle violently fought against the curb until someone could pry open a door and take the driver's foot off the pedal. Men and women were shouting, but I couldn't understand any of it except the occasional pleas to God or his deputized saints. Someone in our group said we needed to leave. A half dozen *ferenj* (foreigners) in the middle of an emotional and expanding crowd was bad. I looked down at the hand I still had on the SUV driver's arm. I let go. My palm itched as if helping him had left a sign on my skin, only visible under some karmic blacklight.

Conflicted, our group got away before more people could show up and possibly blame the white pedestrians or ask for a donation for the minibus driver. This wasn't taken personally. We just stood out as a bunch of white foreigners at a crash site, spot-lit by the fluorescent streetlamp above us. Peace Corps staff tells Volunteers not to get involved in events like this for good reason. Chaotic situations can lead to health risks, such as contact with bodily fluids or personal injury, whether deliberate or not. Scammers, thieves, and opportunists use confusion to coerce money or unsafe actions from bystanders. So, we quickly worked our way back to the hotel and had a drink in the lobby which doubled as the hotel bar.

That evening blurred into the rest of my experiences in Ethiopia. I didn't have more than passing thoughts on it until I was strapped to that backboard in the ambulance trying to remember what year it was. I spent the afternoon in a hospital being evaluated for brain trauma and was eventually released after being diagnosed with a severe concussion. Eight months of physical therapy followed to address whiplash from the crash. Tinnitus and muffled hearing lasted for months. These issues did improve, but I wouldn't learn until a year later that the impact ruptured an eardrum. A doctor said the rupture was significant based on the amount of visible scar tissue. I wouldn't have known had he not asked about the fresh scarring. It was impossible for me to see the damage myself, I had to rely on others to recognize something was wrong. I felt the damage, even heard the damage, but I was oblivious to the new normal inside my own head.

Sometimes we can be so close to a problem that it is difficult to bring it into focus. Sometimes we want to help, but the best thing to do is to walk away. Sometimes we need to acknowledge our own injuries before we try to help others. And sometimes we need to just shut up and listen, even if it hurts.

BLESS THE RAINS DOWN IN AFRICA

"The best thing one can do when it's raining is to let it rain."
—Henry Wadsworth Longfellow

"The continent is too large to describe. It is a veritable ocean, a separate planet, a varied, immensely rich cosmos. Only with the greatest simplification, for the sake of convenience, can we say 'Africa'. In reality, except as a geographical appellation, Africa does not exist."
—Ryszard Kapuściński

It's one of those songs that is nearly impossible not to sing along to once you hear the intro. "Africa" by the 1980s band Toto is a classic of not only the 20th century, but all human history. The song has become a timeless pop culture classic, which pulls generations in with its emotional yearning and dramatic drumming. It has been played and parodied on numerous TV shows and internet memes. In 2019, an artist even created an art installation in the middle of the Namib desert that will play the song on a loop indefinitely, or at least until it gets covered by a drifting sand dune.

The titular line, "I bless the rains down in Africa," is poignant considering the Ethiopian famine in the early 1980s that flooded the world's TV sets with scenes of starving, swollen-bellied children. It spurred the questionably successful *Band Aid*, which raised millions of dollars for famine relief. However, much of that "relief" went to prop up the genocidal and corrupt Derg regime that largely caused the famine in the first place.

Even more surprising may be the fact that the band members had never been to Africa. Co-writer David Paich admitted he based the lyrics off a late-night documentary chronicling the realities of a famine-wracked Africa, saying, "It both moved and appalled me, and the pictures just wouldn't leave my head. I tried to imagine how I'd feel about it if I was there and what I'd do." Jeff Porcaro, the other writer, added, "A white boy is trying to write a song on Africa, but since he's never been there, he can only tell what he's seen on TV or remembers in the past." The imagery in the song is pulled from pleas for help heard from a living room couch and glossy *Natural Geographic* photographs.

The song paints pictures of acacia trees and wildebeest crossing muddy rivers. Heat rising off the dry savannah creating a mirage that hides a pride of lions. Conical mud huts house families of pastoralists and their meager belongings. True, all these things are present in Africa, but they are NOT Africa. Scholars can't even agree on where the name "Africa" came from. Was it a name given by the people who lived on the continent, or was it a name given to it from abroad? Is it from an Egyptian word for "birthplace," is it Greek for "never being cold," is it Latin for "always being sunny," or does it have an unknown meaning from an ancient language that predates all of these?

Africa is an exceptionally diverse continent—commonly associated with both magnificent wilderness and abject poverty. However, that is only a small part of the stories Africa has to tell. Over 3,000 ethnic groups, speaking more than 2,000 languages, have called the continent home for millennia. The famous, fossilized skeleton of Lucy, a hominid living over 3 million years ago, was discovered in Ethiopia. The skeleton was named after the Beatles song "Lucy in the Sky with Diamonds," by a member of the 1974 expedition who found the fossil. Lucy's name in the Amharic language is Dinkenesh, meaning "you are a wonderful woman."

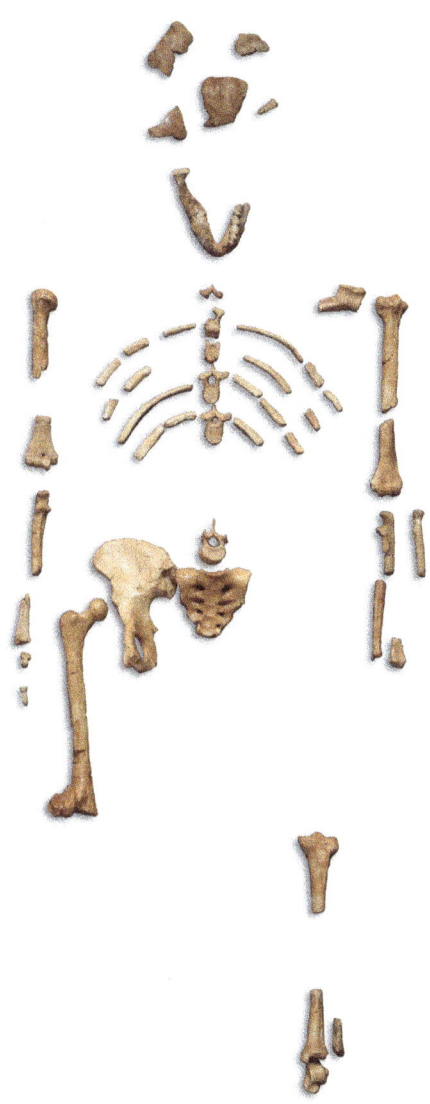

Lucy's fossilized skeleton. Cast from National Museum of Natural History in Paris (120, CC BY-SA 3.0, Wikimedia Commons).

Lucy may appear more ape-like than human, but it is widely accepted by paleontologists that *Homo sapiens* (modern humans) originated in Africa hundreds of thousands of years ago. As of 2023, Ethiopia is home to at least 126 million people, and the population of Africa is nearly 1.5 billion. For comparison, the USA and North America had estimated populations of 340 million and 600 million respectively that same year. Africa has more than double the population of North America, and it is increasing rapidly.

The USA, itself unusually large for a country, is still only a third the size of Africa. Africa truly is massive and currently home to 54 separate countries. The continent has some of the most important, and threatened, ecosystems on Earth. It boasts coral reefs, mountains, deserts, rainforests, grasslands, and nearly everything in between. Nowhere else can you see penguins, lions, wolves, crocodiles, and much more without crossing an ocean…or going to a zoo. Many alphabet books begin and end with Aardvark and Zebra, both naturally found only in Africa.

The dynamic relationship between natural areas such as national parks and the realities of the people who live in or around them are poorly understood. This is due to the extremely complex and changing character of the natural and manmade systems involved. Growing international interest in Africa's natural areas has brought added challenges as policymakers and land managers are forced to balance foreign and domestic calls for conservation or development.

Ethiopia's rapid social and economic development in the past half century has had far-reaching impacts on its protected areas and on people all over the country. The largely rural populations living near these ecological hot spots are dependent on the natural resources in these areas. Natural resources are materials from the Earth that are used to support life and meet people's needs. These include things like water, soil, plants, and animals. Any change in policy or planning can have dramatic impacts on vulnerable people. Frequent changes in government administration and management priorities, and a rapidly growing human population, have weakened Ethiopia's ability to effectively manage these areas. That is the context in which the stories in this book take place.

Ityopia (pronounced Eat-yo-pia) is the Amharic pronunciation of Ethiopia—lacking the "th" sound. The language of the Amharan people is one of the most widely spoken languages in the country. Amharic, or *Amhareñña* in the language, has been the official working language of the Ethiopian government and everyday communications since the late 12th century. It has only been in the past two decades that other languages have been destigmatized at a national level and included as official languages. However, the name *Ityopia* predates even the Amharic language and comes from the combination of Greek words meaning "burnt face," or "reddish-brown," depending on how the original phrase was used. The country's name is an exonym, meaning a non-native word used for a place, language, or people. The name appeared in the famous works of Homer, the celebrated Greek storyteller and scourge of high school literature teachers. Homer used the word in both the *Iliad* and the *Odyssey,* in reference to the land of the "Aethiopians."

Meanwhile, many Ethiopians have adopted the term *Habesha* to refer to all Ethiopians regardless of ethnicity, language, or religion. The origin of this endonym (native word used for a place, language, or people) is as contested as its use. What some Ethiopians view as an empowering, inclusionary name for all Ethiopians, often including Eritreans, others view as a way to divide "true" Ethiopians from imposters. Ultimately, it doesn't matter if someone from the modern country of Ethiopia calls themselves Ityopiawi or Habesha. Rain falls on the "just and unjust" regardless of what they call themselves or others, just as the band Toto did not need to be in Africa to bless the world with a memorable chorus.

PEACE "CORPSE"

*"Life in the Peace Corps will not be easy.
There will be no salary and allowances will be at
a level sufficient only to maintain health and meet basic
needs. Men and women will be expected to work and live
alongside the nationals of the country in which they are
stationed—doing the same work, eating the same food,
talking the same language.
But if the life will not be easy, it will be rich and
satisfying. For every young American who participates in the
Peace Corps—who works in a foreign land—will know that he or
she is sharing in the great common task of bringing to man that
decent way of life which is the foundation of freedom
and a condition of peace."*

—President John F. Kennedy

The flight from the Volunteer trainee staging in Washington DC to Addis Ababa was terrifyingly uneventful. We had spent two days in Washington for staging, a pre-training training. Lengthy orientations, towers of paperwork, and numerous vaccines took their toll. We were ready to get on the plane and become "real" Volunteers. Bright-eyed Peace Corps trainees spent much of the flight standing in the back of the plane trying to decide what our first projects as official PCVs would be. We wouldn't complete our training and be official Volunteers for another three months, but everyone had grand plans for helping the people of Ethiopia. I hardly slept on the flight, and not many from our group were able to close their eyes for more than a few minutes. The rowdy static of our excitement filled the rows we occupied. We were moving to Africa. Our U-Haul truck was a Boeing 777.

I felt proud about going to Africa as a PCV and was certain that the Ethiopian people would not only benefit from the skills I had, but that they would also be grateful for my well-intentioned efforts. I gazed out the airplane window, fantasizing about the opening scene of the biographical film about the inspirational nonprofit I would co-found (because I'm not selfish) following my work in Peace Corps Ethiopia. What a schmuck. At least I was a schmuck in good company. Night caught up with the plane as I looked out the window and pondered what the actor portraying me would say during the plane scene voiceover. I was surprised by the increasing density and brilliance of the lights below us as we came closer to the capital of Ethiopia. These lights carpeted the landscape beneath the airplane in the last few minutes of the flight, and I half wondered whether this was the right place. It seemed too shiny for a country requesting PCVs. I shrugged.

Applying to the Peace Corps had been like writing a note in a bottle and setting it adrift on the sea of federal paperwork—not knowing where it would end up, who would read it, and who would return the bottle with a note of their own. We didn't know what we would be doing, where we would be going, whom we would be going with, or even when we would leave. It was a leap of faith. Months after applying and interviewing, we received a letter in the mail inviting us to serve in Ethiopia. Applying is now more like a traditional job posting with a set location, program, and start date. I'll admit, sometimes I wonder which is better. The mystery and gravity of an unexpected envelope from the Peace Corps head office is difficult to recreate in a boilerplate acceptance email.

Peace Corps (pronounced kor—like Marine Corps) was established by President Kennedy in 1961. Initially created under the US Department of State, it was granted independence as an executive branch agency in 1981. The national Peace Corps "agency" was created with three main goals: (1) to help the people of interested countries in meeting their needs for trained men and women; (2) to help promote a better understanding of Americans on the part of the people served; and (3) to help promote a better understanding of other peoples on the part of all Americans. These three goals can be simplified as:

- Build local capacity
- Share America with the world
- Bring the world home

This book is an attempt at that third goal.

Peace Corps is directly translated as *Yaselam Guad*, which literally means "the body of peace" in Amharic. This is as good a translation as any, but many Ethiopians prefer to call it by its English name. As a syllabic language that functions without freeloading silent letters, many Amharic speakers pronounced it as Peace Corpse—as in a dead body. Although understandable, this occasionally led to confusion by Americans and Ethiopians alike.

Ethiopia was one of the first countries to host PCVs, beginning service in 1962, just one year after the program was announced by JFK. The first Volunteers assisted with educational and health projects in the country. Peace Corps was forced to evacuate Volunteers following the military coup in the 1970s that overthrew the Ethiopian emperor Haile Selassie. And again,

Peace Corps ten-year-anniversary stamp issued in 1972.

Volunteers were evacuated in the late 1990s due to the Eritrean-Ethiopian War (1998–2000). PCVs were only permitted back into Ethiopia in 2007 due to continued border skirmishes between Ethiopia and its former state, Eritrea. Unfortunately, Peace Corps was forced to leave yet again in 2020 due to the COVID-19 pandemic and rising tensions between the federal Ethiopian government and the Tigray state, located on Eritrea's southern border.

The Tigray War (2020–2022) surprisingly brought together the Ethiopian and Eritrean militaries against the Tigrayan ethnic group, in retaliation for ethnic crimes from the civil war and the internal political grudges that followed. Tigray gained political power through its military prowess against Eritrea during the Ethiopian Civil War (1974–1991). The Tigray People's Liberation Front (TPLF), the primary political party representing Tigray, dominated national politics after the civil war, despite Tigrayans' status as an ethnic minority, making up only about 5% of the national population. Nearly three decades of Tigray dominance in Ethiopia's government soured many fellow Ethiopians on the region and its people.

Dr. Abiy Ahmed, from the populous Oromo ethnic group, was elected prime minister in 2018 and put an end to Tigrayan hegemony. Before he was elected, the country was led by a coalition of four dominant political parties called the Ethiopian People's Revolutionary Democratic Front (EPRDF). This coalition included the TPLF, but also included the Amhara Democratic Party (ADP), Oromo Democratic Party (ODP), and Southern Ethiopian People's Democratic Movement (SEPDM). Each party represented a different ethnic group; or, in the case of SEPDM, dozens of ethnic groups. Prime Minister Abiy dissolved this coalition government in 2019 and created a new political party to replace the ethnicity-based parties of the past. The previously powerful

TPLF looked down on this political cohabitation and refused to join. However, the other three parties from the coalition joined a half-dozen other political groups from around the country to form a new "Prosperity Party." Animosity of the TPLF was, and is, one of the strongest glues holding this pan-Ethiopian party together. This is especially true of the governments in the neighboring Oromia and Amhara states. They fundamentally disagreed with each other, which was fine as long as they each disagreed with Tigray more.

Prime Minister Abiy was a seemingly ideal selection for reconciling the country's fractious government. A decorated child soldier who fought against the Marxist Derg regime, Abiy became a military intelligence officer during the war with Eritrea but left military service in 2010 to become a politician. His father was Muslim, and his mother was Christian, which gave him an understanding of the two largest religious groups in the country of then 90 million people. His fluency in Tigrayan, Oromo, Amharic, and English allowed personal communication with nearly three quarters of Ethiopians.

With a reputation as a skilled negotiator, Abiy was awarded the 2019 Nobel Peace Prize for his efforts to resolve the border conflict with Eritrea. However, the Tigray War broke out less than a year after he received the prestigious award. The conflict took the lives of thousands of federalists and Tigrayans. War crimes were committed by all sides involved—no hands were clean. COVID-19, the exclusion and arrest of journalists, and global preoccupation with American politics shielded the world from the horrors experienced by civilians and soldiers. As of 2024, the fog of war and ongoing security concerns still prevent Ethiopia from hosting PCVs. Tigray hosted hundreds of Volunteers throughout Peace Corps Ethiopia's history, but the region is now a recovering war zone, scattered with mass graves and thousands of displaced people. It will take decades for the Tigray state to rebuild, and that assumes no further violence.

The Peace Corps Ethiopia Conservation and Natural Resource Management program began with my cohort in September 2010. Volunteers were placed in the then "stable" Ethiopian states of Tigray, Amhara, Oromia, as well as Southern Nations, Nationalities and Peoples Region (SNNPR). This was the first conservation-focused program that the Peace Corps attempted in Ethiopia.

The wide-eyed group of Americans was dispersed to our respective sites after a ten-week training that included lessons in the language, culture, and environmental issues. About a third of trainees, including my wife and I, were partnered with the Ethiopian Wildlife Conservation Authority (EWCA), the national agency responsible for managing the country's national parks and their wildlife. The original goals of the program were to: improve the livelihood of communities residing in the buffer zone of protected areas; improve environmental knowledge in urban and rural communities; and facilitate operations in Ethiopia's national parks.

Subsequent groups of Volunteers would focus more on sustainable agriculture in Ethiopia. This was partially due to changing needs in the country, but primarily due to the unrealistic expectations of our Ethiopian partners. By the end of our two-year service, only one Volunteer from our group had a "successful" project with EWCA. The agency administration expected PCVs to be funders, not capacity-builders and program designers. However, Volunteers didn't receive any funding aside from small living allowances. I, and many others, pursued modest grants and private funding opportunities for the projects we worked on. EWCA was looking for multimillion-dollar support that we simply couldn't provide.

When PCVs arrive at their post, they are faced with the

challenge of identifying and prioritizing projects that build on their host community's capacity to solve self-identified problems. They are required to complete a Community Needs Assessment within their first few months at their host sites. This is an action-focused report meant to provide Volunteers with a better understanding of the communities they will live in for two years. The goal is for Volunteers to create a working document that helps their host communities select actionable ideas and access the resources needed to carry them out. The report is intended to highlight the experiences and knowledge of communities as much as it is to find problems to solve. The process of co-creating the report creates opportunities for Volunteers and host communities to develop rapport and understand each other's needs and expectations.

This is all much easier said than done. Implementing projects in a foreign country is time consuming, requiring patience and an openness to cultural differences. Working with unfamiliar institutions using a new language, while navigating a foreign culture, is a challenge for PCVs worldwide.

SHIT AND SUGARCANE

"And for all its irritations, frustrations, and humiliations, illness may teach us all something of value, even if that thing is only to cherish health when we have it, or see it in others. [...] From time to time, we all need to learn the art of convalescence."
—Gavin Francis

"Life would pall if it were all sugar; salt is bitter if taken by itself; but when tasted as part of the dish, it savours the meat. Difficulties are the salt of life."
—Robert Baden-Powell

President Girme Walde-Girogis was a morbidly obese man in a country whose name is globally synonymous with famine. Despite his weight, he passed away from natural causes in 2018, at the age of 93. The Ethiopian presidency is mostly ceremonial because power is held by the prime minister instead. Regardless, Girme was an environmentalist, humanitarian, and fierce public servant. He attended the swearing-in ceremony that saw me sworn-in as an official PCV. It's not every day that you shake the hand of such an important government official, just as it's not every day that you shit yourself. Both are significant events, but never so significant as when they happen on the same day.

The Volunteer trainees in our group went through an intensive ten-week training program before we could become bona fide Volunteers. We lived with host families, ate with host families, and did laundry with host families—learning skills we would need for the next two years. This included emergency latrine-locating skills. Host families often don't understand the need for bodies to acclimate to new foods and environments because many never left the village they were born in. They drank the water from their well when they were children, why would a grown adult have a problem drinking it? When they have a stomachache, they drink copious amounts of buttered coffee (you read that right, buttered) and eat hot peppers. The toxic, bitter seed pods of common rue, a shrubby herb, are popped like Tylenol. Called *Tenadam*, meaning "Adam's health," the rue plant is an Ethiopian cure-all. Why wouldn't a ferenj have the same tastes and medical needs?

It would be an understatement to say most trainees experienced "intestinal discomfort" at some point during training. I was sick most of the three-months, but it was not until the last three weeks that I suspected I was going to die. I had always been lanky. However, whatever small amount of body fat I had

The latrine at Derek and Claire's pre-service training site.

quickly disappeared, along with what seemed like all the moisture in my body—mostly through its back end. I lost nearly 60 pounds, a third of my body weight, as well as most of my attempts to reach the latrine on time. A common Peace Corps Ethiopia saying is, "Every fart's a gamble." I never was good at gambling, and the saying gives new meaning to the term crapshoot.

My illness likely resulted from contaminated well water. Our host family had dug their well concerningly close to their pit latrine. We boiled and filtered all the water that came anywhere close to our faces. However, our hosts rinsed plates and utensils in untreated water pulled from the open well with a plastic bucket. I was unable to eat solid food for over two weeks and could only sip enough water to wet my mouth without vomiting. The alarming weight loss and dehydration earned me a trip to the Peace Corps medical offices in Addis Ababa.

A saline IV drip and Oral Rehydration Salts (ORS) made me feel human again—like I could do more than just sleep and shit myself. The ORS tasted like Capri-Sun marketed to saltwater fish. But it restored my lost electrolytes. Inappropriately dubbed "ghetto-rade," these salty drinks save lives. My sunken eyes caught the rising tide and floated back into place like ocean buoys. My sore joints drank greedily, and the endless headache weakened to a mild static crackle. I was tired of lying down for days and had to fight the urge to stand up. I let the water flow into my body while the medical lab tested the involuntarily copious stool samples I provided. The Peace Corps physician came to give me the results the next morning.

"Well, there are two main types of dysentery—amoebic and bacterial. Neither are pleasant," he began in droll doctor-speak.

"OK, which one do I have?"

He paused, acting like it should be obvious, and glanced

quickly at a clipboard for confirmation. "Both," he answered, a little too upbeat.

Peace Corps gave me an antibiotic and antiparasitic drug cocktail, which I took before returning to my hotel room to sleep as long as I could. The remaining doses were in the paper bag I casually dropped on the floor on the way to bed. The dunes in my gut shifted while I slept, and I woke with the now familiar sense of urgency. I felt broken as I stripped naked and climbed into the bathtub. Nature was left to take its course, from both ends, as I laid there—occasionally turning on the shower to clean myself. It took three tries and as many hours, to keep down the second dose of medication.

The swearing-in ceremony was the next day, and I started to feel better without needing an IV in my arm. I woke, got dressed, and nursed my breakfast of sweetened salt water. I joined the other trainees on the bus that took us to the fortified US Embassy compound where the ceremony was going to take place. The cramps in my stomach got worse the closer we got to the embassy. I couldn't ignore them any longer as we pulled up to the sizable security gate. Finally!

The relief of arriving weakened the concentration needed to keep what was inside me from being on the outside of me. I lost the gamble, and I lost badly. Despite not eating solid food for weeks, my body found enough material to leave no doubt what had just happened. I sat petrified as two security guards climbed on the bus and asked for our passports one by one. In an act of divine mercy, the guards got bored about halfway down the bus and waved us through without checking everyone. The bus parked, but I hesitated as everyone stood to leave. Now what?

I stood clumsily and tried not to look at the small dark spot on the seat behind me as I walked off the bus. I was too terrified and embarrassed to let anyone know and asked a guard for a bathroom as soon as my foot hit the pavement. In addition to the trainees being sworn in and a small army of security personnel, several hundred people were in attendance. Most were embassy staff or guests from other government offices. In an act of almost criminal negligence, the people in charge of planning the event didn't anticipate at least one of these attendees needing a restroom during the ceremony and buffet that followed. The closest "public restroom" was in the main office building a quarter mile and several security checkpoints away. I was struggling just standing there. I wasn't going to make it.

After several minutes of confused looks, and "Oh yeah, I'm not sure where the bathroom is," I was shuffled toward the ambassador's mansion, flanked by three heavily armed security officers and the ambassador's wife. "My husband and I, and everyone here at the embassy, are so proud of your hard work. We are very excited to see what Ethiopia has in store for you," she said genuinely. We stopped at the mansion entrance where she shook my hand and left back down the large marble steps.

Two stone-faced Marines opened the monstrous front door and pointed me to the opposite end of the foyer as I stepped inside. I assumed the Marines were mistaken because the door I was directed toward looked like it should be to a broom closet. I tentatively opened the door and flipped on the light. It was a bathroom, but barely large enough for a single sink and toilet. The room was dwarfed by the rooms surrounding it, but right then it was the single most important room in the mansion. I felt awful, but still couldn't help a chuckle. I was now standing in the ambassador's entry bathroom, naked except for muddy shoes and a traditional Ethiopian white shirt, cleaning blood and bile out of my ExOfficio boxers. I considered throwing the boxers away, but realized they might be needed again and cleaned them the best I could.

I splashed water on my face and toweled it dry before leaving the bathroom. I knocked on the front door. The Marines outside opened it, and I thanked them quickly before leaving. I didn't want to miss shaking hands with the president of Ethiopia because I took too long cleaning myself. I had no reason to hurry because the president was running late, and we ended up waiting another hour before the ceremony began. The ceremony crept along as only diplomatic, public relations events can. Eventually, trainees were called up one by one to get a certificate and shake the president's hand. I was ten people away from being called when the all-too-familiar cramps started again, and I was glad I decided to keep my boxers. I was four people away from being called when I gambled and lost for the second time that day. I had experienced all the stages of grief by the time I stood up, accepted my certificate, shook the president's hand, and sat back down again.

Poop was a daily fact of life in Ethiopia. It was everywhere. Cow, horse, dog, and human were all well represented in plain sight when walking around rural towns. Cow dung was less common because it was collected to use as plaster in traditional buildings or dried as cooking fuel. Flush toilets were rare, often only found in hotels with private bathrooms. Most people used pit latrines or just found a convenient place to go. The most convenient places were usually in open fields or alongside fences.

No attempt was made to clean up or even hastily cover the *berbere* spice-crusted coils baking like malformed bricks in the equatorial sun. In the dry season, they withered within a day, got trampled into coarse powder by hooves, paws, and feet, which then got picked up by warm breezes and joined the dust, coating everything. It invaded the eyes, nose, and mouth. A poorly timed conversation on the side of the road could require gargling water afterward. In the rainy season, the consistency of

Derek and Claire dressed for the Peace Corps swearing-in ceremony at the US Embassy.

the mud under your feet became suspect, and the sight of children splashing in puddles could churn your stomach. Thankfully, even in small villages, cane sugar-sweetened sodas were always available to wash the taste away—even if served warm.

However, oil and sugar shortages were common in rural Ethiopia. I inadvertently started a small riot when I bought a ration of cooking oil from the local government office that was intended for someone else. Local Ethiopian cuisine could grind to a halt without copious amounts of imported palm oil. There were some domestically produced oils available, but their small harvests could not compete with cheap, imported oil. Just as Ethiopian food struggled without oil, Ethiopian drinks struggled without sugar. Tea and coffee were usually taken with seemingly equal parts sugar and liquid. These drinks were served with respect for the recipient, but their sweetness could surpass the most diabetes-inducing soft drinks. Some local restaurants didn't bother serving tea or coffee when the town's sugar supply dried up for over a week. Tea without sugar was fit for beggars and the mentally ill who relied on charity to survive.

"What is the relationship between shit and sugar?" you may ask. Well, they aren't connected except by their ubiquity in the daily life of a foreigner living in rural Africa. Sure, manure fertilizes sugarcane, and sugarcane eventually turns back into manure in a circle of life kind of way, but I apologize if you were expecting this to be a bittersweet analogy of life as a PCV in Africa. Life in rural Africa can defy logical connections because it is so different from what most people in the Global North have experienced. Life in Africa is…life in Africa. It can feel like a standardized test that can only be correctly answered by the people who wrote the test. You take the test knowing you will get most of the answers wrong, sure as shit—and sugarcane.

THREADING THE NEEDLE(S)

"I do not hate Africa or the Africans. What I hate is the senseless brutality, the waste of human life. I hate the unfairness, the injustice, the way repressive systems strip decent people of their dignity. [...] Perhaps more than that, I hate this maddening propensity of Africans to wallow in their own suffering, to simply roll over when kicked, and to express unswerving faith that some outside force, some divine intervention, will bring deliverance from their misery."

—Keith B. Richburg

"But African time was not the same as American time... As African time passed, I surmised that the pace of Western countries was insane, that the speed of modern technology accomplished nothing, and that because Africa was going its own way at its own pace for its own reasons, it was a refuge and a resting place."

—Paul Theroux

Ethiopia has a reputation among development organizations for its highly bureaucratic and strictly regulated governmental structure. Not necessarily corrupt, but grueling to navigate. This way of functioning is ingrained in Ethiopian culture and is the result of hundreds of years of authoritarian rule; most notably from the oppressive Derg regime from 1974 to 1991. As a result, many government employees have become paperwork despots, duty-bound to inactivity unless otherwise directed by a superior. This involves multiple copies, multiple personalized stamps, and multiple requests for the same information. Programs and individual projects operate at different government levels, and often at more than one level. When planning a project in Ethiopia, it is important to decide which government offices you want involved and to predict which may become involved before the project is completed.

As conservation-focused PCVs, one of our expected duties was to distribute information about fuel-efficient wood stoves and to promote their adoption in our community. In college, my wife and I interned at a nonprofit that did excellent work with such stoves. Therefore, we were excited and felt well-equipped to work on fuel-efficient stove programs. I was even selected to present Peace Corps stove projects to the Administrator of the US Environmental Protection Agency at an event in Addis Ababa

Common Ethiopian kitchen setup for cooking over open fire. Years of soot coat the walls.

while she was touring Africa. We left the highly publicized event energized and very ready to promote stoves in the Simien Mountains. These stoves would allow people to save money by buying less firewood and also improve their health by reducing air pollution from smoky open fires.

The mountains were once covered in native forests. Trees were cut down for firewood centuries before the modern nation of Ethiopia even existed. The landscape around the town we served in was once covered in African redwood trees. The area was originally called Kosso Mender, meaning "Redwood Village" in Amharic. Its name was changed to Debark in the 16th century, a fitting name for a place that cut down all its trees.

The excitement about our stove assignment quickly cooled as we faced the reality of being fundless foreigners trying to work in Ethiopia. We met with local agricultural extension workers and stove makers to help promote the fuel-efficient stove designs. We learned the current stove design was too expensive for many people to afford and was not well-suited to the cultural idiosyncrasies of using open fires for cooking, warmth, and light in the Ethiopian highlands. We found a more appropriate stove design that was being promoted by the German development agency GIZ, which is short for German Development Cooperation in German.

After weeks of phone calls, and meeting with a GIZ representative in the nearby city of Gondar, we had an agreement with GIZ to come to Debark and provide a week-long stove training. Local farmers would learn to gather construction materials, build the stoves, and market them in the surrounding area. The farmers would be paid to attend the training and given start-up capital to develop an association of stove manufacturers. All this funding would be provided by GIZ. The local government only needed to identify farmers who wanted to be involved and to collect the initial construction materials which GIZ would reimburse them for.

Instead, the local government demanded a formal letter from the Director of GIZ stating exactly what the training was for and implying that GIZ must pay the local administration an unspecified amount of money to host the training. After many weeks of trying to negotiate between the local government and GIZ, we gave up. GIZ staff were understandably not interested in going out of their way to provide a paid training if the local government would make demands and question intentions.

We discussed the situation with friends in town, and it became apparent that these difficulties were not uncommon. The local government often charged an "altruism tax" on organizations or even groups of tourists who wanted to donate to a particular project or cause. A group of tourists once expressed interest in building a deep well for a community that lived in the buffer zone of the national park. While trekking in the park, they saw young girls traveling miles over mountainous terrain to bring water to their families. When the tourists brought their proposal to a local government administrator, he told them the well would cost over three times the actual amount due to fees and administrative oversight. Remote wells are not inexpensive to begin with, and the tourists balked at the inflated price. The well was never built, and the young granddaughters of those girls are still hauling water. The park guide who told me about the well project wrung his hands through his close-cropped hair and told me that he was afraid of getting arrested if I implicated him by repeating the story in public.

Such issues are not unique to Debark. They are nested in nearly every level of Ethiopian government. At the national level is the Federal Democratic Republic of Ethiopia, with its multitude of ministries and institutions. When speaking about conservation, this is often represented by the Ethiopian Wildlife Conservation Authority (EWCA) or the Ministry of Agriculture. At the state level is the Amhara National Regional State (ANRS) with its own state offices based on federal ministries. The third level is the zonal level, which breaks down states into more manageable areas. These divisions may be ethnic or geographical. Zonal duties are often delegated to the *Woreda* (county) level. The zonal government is a mosaic of numerous Woredas and acts as an intermediary between state and county governments. Each Woreda typically has one or more "urban" areas, which are market towns or large villages. The Woreda level brings the nested structure of state government offices down to the local level. Each Woreda has a Manager who is the hand of the ruling party in local matters.

An abandoned Armored Personnel Carrier outside the Debark administration building.

Lastly, each Woreda is composed of numerous *Kebele*. The Kebele is the smallest division of Ethiopian governance and is at the village or neighborhood level. Each Kebele controls government policy on a personal level. Almost all Ethiopians have regular interaction with the government at this level because it oversees local permitting and documentation. The Kebele is sometimes broken into sub-Kebeles, which are composed of 30 to 90 households. However, these sub-Kebele divisions are not used for administrative functions, but rather to extend government control to an even more personal level. They are a vestigial form of governance from Ethiopia's autocratic past.

Are you confused? I wouldn't feel like I had done a good job explaining the government hierarchy unless you were. Each government level has advantages and disadvantages for working with...or around. The size of each level, office locations, and opportunities for personal contact with decision-makers make it difficult to generalize. The federal level exerts power by directing policy and deciding what is allowed by lower offices. Some departments, such as EWCA, only have decision-makers at their federal headquarters. Working with federal level staff can be extremely difficult because certain issues will only be discussed face-to-face. These issues require a personal trip to Addis Ababa for decisions to be made or approved. C.W. Nicol, the young British man who served as the park's first game warden in the 1970s, lamented,

> "I could go blue in the face telling a government official that the Simien [park] was beautiful, but if he hadn't seen it, and didn't want to see it, it was hard to win him over to the conservationist's point of view. To most of those officials, progress meant fine buildings in the capital, not a lot of animals running around in the bush, making a nuisance of themselves in the crops."

The local EWCA offices, such as the SMNP office, are slow to act on issues they don't have previous experience with. This is understandable. However, working with these offices necessitates networking with staff from the head office in Addis Ababa. This limits access to the relevant EWCA "trigger-person," the person who has the authority and the interest to take the initial actions that move a project beyond casual meetings and make it a reality. In other words, people who can pull the trigger to get a project out of the barrel and on target.

States in Ethiopia function much like states in the USA. The 1994 constitution announced the establishment of nine Ethiopian states, each based on "settlement patterns, language, identity, and consent of the peoples concerned." The state level of government takes its cues from the federal government but has some autonomy in its decision-making. The state government, however, is awkwardly placed between management on a national level and on a local level. Authority for projects is often placed above or below state leaders, with veto power being a preferred way of flexing the authority they have.

The Woreda level is the main decision-maker on most local projects. Their decisions can be overridden from a higher office, but this often requires a very close relationship with someone on the next step up the ladder. Even seemingly trivial issues get brought to the Woreda administration for review. Each Kebele is an extension of the Woreda. The Woreda is a hand, and Kebeles are its fingers. It can be easier to ask Kebele managers to facilitate a project because the Kebeles function at a much more personal and accessible level. Assuming one has the right connections, it can be relatively easy to make (small) things happen at the Kebele level.

The federal level is wrapped in red tape and can be difficult to navigate unless someone with enough authority can make introductions. This, combined with a strong sense of self-importance, can make attempting work at this level unrewarding. Working at the state level can be easier than federal because of its relative autonomy from federal authority and the smaller geography being managed. Implementing projects with the cooperation of Woreda offices can create a perfect storm of definitive authority, egos, and fear of stepping on the toes of the people above them.

These different levels act as sieves, stopping or slowing programs and projects. Some may say this is an unfair generalization of development projects in Ethiopia and that these administrative tiers are opportunities for host country participation. This can be true, but such rose-tinted glasses become heavy if left on too long. A government official will probably not get in trouble from a higher authority for stopping or slowing a project's progress, but it is possible they would get in trouble for allowing a project to continue. Patience, persistence, and realistic goals improve the chances of a project being successful. A large budget helps too.

WELCOME TO DEBARK

"Leaving home in a sense involves a kind of second birth in which we give birth to ourselves."
—Robert Neelly Bellah

"Community offers the promise of belonging and calls for us to acknowledge our interdependence. To belong is to act as an investor, owner, and creator of this place. To be welcome even if we are strangers. [...] To feel a sense of belonging is important because it will lead us from conversations about safety and comfort to other conversations, such as our relatedness and willingness to provide hospitality and generosity."
—Peter Block

"*Solomon neyn*," I told the guard as I shook his hand, "I am Solomon." He nodded as if this was the expected answer and turned to look at Claire standing beside me. "This is my wife," I said in Amharic. "Her name is Ababa."

His face lit up as he opened the gate. "These are Ethiopian names. Very good! Go inside."

We thanked him and walked into the high-walled compound housing the Debark Town government offices. We were grateful to the national park scout who had gifted us Habesha names. My English name has a meaning in Amharic, and it isn't positive. *Derek* means "stubborn, stiff, and dry." It is meant to communicate mental inflexibility or a lack of something. However, mentioning this when introducing myself was a self-insulting icebreaker that never failed to get an appreciative laugh. Claire's name didn't mean anything in Amharic but was difficult to pronounce for many people. *Ababa*, meaning "flower," was easy for both Ethiopians and foreigners to pronounce, and was a traditional name.

We had come to the town offices to introduce ourselves and feel out potential partnerships with the local government. This was the fourth time we had tried to get a meeting with town administrators since moving to Debark and, after a long wait, were able to meet the middle-aged "elders" who worked there. We never were able to find a project to work on with the town officials, but at least now they knew the names of these random white people living there.

Our original host site was located roughly 10mi (16km) from Debark, near the main gate to SMNP. We quickly realized the small community there was too isolated to conduct projects because it was located an hour into the park and not accessible by vehicle. Strict Peace Corps policies on Volunteers using transportation made buying food and supplies difficult. Our initial treks to the village were enjoyable and hospitable. Unfortunately, the projects the community wanted were neither practical nor affordable. The village wanted to expand its impressive network of aqueducts made from dugout eucalyptus logs and to pump irrigation water to the grasslands on a plateau hundreds of feet above. After six weeks living inside the park, we were compelled to move to Debark, where we stayed for the remainder of our two-year Peace Corps term of service.

Debark and Debark Town were interchangeable in Ethiopia. Designation as a "Town" in Amharic indicates that the settlement is larger than a village, but smaller than a county, which may all share the same name. Debark's unique name is a combination of Amharic words for "agreement" and "prowl." The name implies that an agreement was made, but that it was meant to hide a malicious agenda. It is a fitting name for a market town that has housed numerous faiths, armies, and merchants over a span of millennia. A more succinct translation would be, "it's not fair." Warden C.W. Nicol, would agree. He described Debark as,

> "the dirtiest, ugliest, town I had ever seen. Wherever we stopped, men and children gathered around to stare [...] this was a dark, seemingly hostile stare [...] Debark was crowded, with many people on mules or horses, and others strutting around with their rifles and bandoliers, arrogant as fighting cocks."

Much is different, but also exactly the same. Debark is a boom town. In only a decade, from 2000 to 2010, the town went from a village recovering from a costly civil war to being the gateway to one of Ethiopia's most visited national parks. Since 2010, the main road that was once packed clay is now a well-trafficked, paved road. An overgrazed pasture leading into town is now a small, modern university. The area has been flooded by domestic and foreign investment hoping to strike it rich on this Ethiopian gold rush. Ethiopians and foreigners, mostly from Europe, have tried to stake a claim on the gold in tourists' pockets by developing services for tourists in Debark and northern Ethiopia in general. These efforts have been stymied by the COVID-19 pandemic and ongoing conflicts in the neighboring Tigray Region.

Before the Italian occupation during World War II (WWII) (1936–1941), Debark was a small rural settlement that had importance as a customs station, caravan stop, and centralized market town. The town itself sits at an elevation of 9,350ft (2,850m) above sea level. Its past and current development is dependent on its location between the ancient cultural centers of

Castle ruins in Gondar that survived Italian bombings in WWII.

Axum, Lalibela, and Gondar. Debark's location in the volcanic mountain range made it a convenient rest stop for long-distance travelers.

The Simien Mountains have sheltered groups of refugees, criminals, and armed forces for millennia due to their ruggedness. The first recorded inhabitants were Ethiopian Jews, but many either converted to the Ethiopian Orthodox faith or migrated following a failed rebellion in the 15th century. This rebellion was put down during a battle between Gondar and Debark. These Jews became known as *Falasha* or "homeless," which understandably has some negative connotations. Currently, the area is dominated by Orthodox Christians and Muslims.

Because the Simien Mountains are encircled by ancient cultural centers, trade routes grew and have greatly influenced the development of the area for the past two thousand years. A local dialect called *Samenteñña* developed, a freestyle mix of primarily Amharic (*Amhareñña*), Tigrayan (*Tigreñña*), and a little Ge'ez, an ancient language which their alphabets are based on. They sound similar yet unique, like comparing Spanish and Portuguese. Such mixed languages are called *Guramayle* in Amharic. The name comes from the ancient practice of tattooing an alternating pattern on the inside of the mouth using needles and soot. The Amharic script combines 7 vowels with 33 consonants to create a mind-numbing 231 characters. Imagine having an alphabet with nearly ten times as many letters as you have now. However, once someone learns these letters, they will be able to pronounce any word in any of these languages because the script is syllabic. They may not know what the words mean, but they can at least pronounce them correctly. Each letter forms a complete sound.

The ebb and flow of people through the mountains has led to overlapping place names and jumbled translations. For example, a massive pair of stone spires called *Imet Gogo* (alternatively spelled *Emetgogo, Mietgogo, Metagogo*, etc.) is one of the most popular places to photograph in the park. If you were to ask a visitor what they were told the name was, they might say a guide told them it means "beautiful place," "bread of truth," or "my mother" if confused with *Inatye*, another famous viewpoint. My favorite, however, is "diarrhea biscuit."

Interestingly, a dash of Italian was added during the First Italo-Ethiopian War in the 1890s, which put Italy's conquest of East Africa on hold until the Second Italo-Ethiopian War in the 1930s. Ethiopia's last emperor Haile Sellasie I was named *Time Magazine*'s Man of the Year in 1935 for his resistance to Italy.

This war with Italy was the often-ignored preamble to WWII. The war saw newly minted German dictator Adolf Hitler supplying Ethiopia with just enough weaponry to bog down Italy in Africa and manipulate Italian dictator Benito Mussolini into supporting Germany's expansionist plans for Europe. This gambit paid off for Hitler, but Ethiopia was stuck in a chaotic conflict with Italian forces until September 1943, when Italy bowed out of WWII and gave up its dreams of an African empire. The Italian occupation was a brutal period for Ethiopia that cost tens of thousands of lives. However, Italy left behind traces of its culture in roads, language, foods, animal breeds, and most importantly—the macchiato coffee.

Samuel Gobat, a Swiss explorer who traveled through Ethiopia in the early 1800s, considered Debark's market to be one of the greatest in Ethiopia because hundreds of people came every week from Gondar to exchange animals and cloth for salt and other exotic goods. An important Italian customs outpost was established in Debark due to its position near the notoriously difficult Wulkifit (now commonly called Limalimo) Pass, which was the northern imperial border in the 17th century. The tortuous Italian-built road through the pass has made travel easier, but the views are no less awe-inspiring.

During the Italian occupation, the highway constructed between Addis Ababa and Asmara, the Eritrean Capital, granted Debark even more importance as a regional economic hotspot. This highway enters Debark south from Gondar and leaves north toward the Limalimo Pass. This section of the highway represents the leg between Gondar and Axum on the Historic Tourism Circuit in the Amhara region. Instead of selling livestock and textiles, now the local economy is dominated by selling Ethiopian culture and spectacular views of the Simien Mountains to tourists.

The large open-air market is still the hub of Debark but is

Emperor Haile Selassie "King of Kings" on the cover of Time Magazine, *November 3, 1930.*

now surrounded by permanent shops. These eclectic shops are as diverse as the items they sell. A small wattle-and-daub shack sells plastic wash basins right next to a modern cinder block building selling the latest failed fashion trends from China. Some vendors hang examples of their wares near their doorways to advertise what they sell. Many businesses maintain the same customers for years, or even generations. Such loyal customers, called *dabeñña,* may get reduced prices or faster service for frequenting that shop. The small shops, called *souks,* regularly sell the exact same things as the surrounding shops. Price collusion is common among vendors because they want to keep the peace with long-term neighbors, yet still make money.

Since price varies so little, and patronage is based on relationships, advertising has never been a large part of going to market. However, that is changing. Paved roads and regional airports have made it drastically easier to travel and transport products. Vendors and customers have more options than ever before, and that is changing the face of Debark's once timeless

Derek buying supplies from a souk while dogs (Tikuru and Titi) stand guard.

market. For example, one café owner had a sign made by their son as a project for their Computer Design class in university. As a result, generic clip art and misspelled English words in blocky fonts cover miniature billboards throughout town. The traditional customer loyalties don't exist for foreign, or even domestic, visitors. Without a dabeñña shopkeeper, visitors need signs to direct them to vendors selling what non-repeat customers need at a fair (enough) price.

Debark is home to the head office of SMNP, the most visited national park in Ethiopia and a major international tourist attraction in the country. The park is alternatively spelled Samen, Simen, Semien, Semyen or Semen, due to the syllabic structure of the Amharic language and differing pronunciations for the mountain range. This can become confusing and even alarming for visitors as they pass a sign for "Semen Coffee." All the spellings, however, mean "north" in Amharic, and the mountain range is known by Ethiopians as The Northern Mountains. The Simien spelling is phonetically closest to the local pronunciation of the name.

The name of the mountains reveals their long-standing cultural importance for Ethiopians. As previously mentioned, Amharic developed from the ancient Semitic language of Ge'ez. Ge'ez was spoken in the Kingdom of Axum which once covered much of East Africa and Southern Arabia. Ge'ez can be thought of as a kind of Ethiopian Latin—a historical language now primarily used by intellectuals and religious purists. The Simien Mountains are south of the ancient city of Axum. In Ge'ez, the word Simien originally meant south, not north. As the center of Ethiopian civilization shifted from Axum southward toward Lalibela, then Gondar, then Addis Ababa, the mountains became a constant reference for the language and identity of the entire Ethiopian Empire. The Simien Mountains, now north of most of the

Ethiopian nobility, came to mean north instead of south. These mountains were the pivot point for an entire language, culture, and empire.

Established in 1966, but not formally recognized until 1969, SMNP was Ethiopia's first national park. Based on its importance to biodiversity and its exceptional beauty, it became one of the first United Nations Educational, Scientific and Cultural Organization (UNESCO) World Heritage Sites when it was inscribed on the World Heritage List in 1978. The park has gone through several changes in its boundaries since its original mapping, and estimates of the park's exact size vary. At the time it was established, the park covered 53mi^2 (137km^2) but has since expanded to 187mi^2 (484km^2). The park will be discussed in depth in later chapters.

DEEP ROOTS

"The tree is more than first a seed, then a stem, then a living trunk, and then dead timber. The tree is a slow, enduring force straining to win the sky."
—Antoine de Saint-Exupéry

"To be without trees would, in the most literal way, to be without our roots."
—Richard Mabey

Our neighbors in Debark, Dinkenesh and Asmara, were the first to invite us over to share a meal. It came the day right after moving into our house, and it was the first of many such visits. The invitation to share a meal would usually be left open to whatever time we wanted to come over. But they would sometimes specify a time if it was a special occasion, such as a holiday meal. We would always have to clarify if they meant Ethiopian time or "foreigner" time. Ethiopian time is calculated from 6AM when the sun rises. Being so close to the equator, there is very little difference in day length throughout the year. So, instead of starting at midnight, the hours start at sunrise.

When I say it was an invitation to "share a meal," I mean it in a very literal sense. Ethiopian food is meant to be shared. Meals are typically served on a single large platter from which everyone that is present eats, or at least as many people that can fit around the platter. Again, I mean very literally as many people as possible that can fit. For example, if you think the number of men that can use a single urinal is one, you are incorrect. The correct answer is five. Similar to eating at an Ethiopian table—as many as can physically squeeze next to each other.

The platter is completely covered by a single large piece of *injera*, a sort of sourdough crepe that is both plate, napkin, and eating utensil. This light and deliciously sour bread is traditionally made with teff, but many Ethiopian households have begun making injera with cheaper grains, such as wheat and barley. The main meal of various stews is poured onto the injera and pieces of the bread are torn off to scoop them up.

Before you can begin eating, it is appropriate to wash your hands at the table. Traditionally, a child or woman carries a pitcher of water and wash basin to each person. Everyone takes turns wringing their hands together as the person pours water over them, allowing it to collect in the basin below. This was usually done by our 19-year-old neighbor Selam.

Dinkenesh, Selam's aunt, was only a couple of years older than us, but made a show of giving us a *gorsha*. Pinching a piece of injera between her fingers, she would grab as much food as possible in the edible pouch and shove the whole thing into our mouths. This is a sign of respect and friendship, but it often ends in laughter and a modest mess. Claire and I would often do it to each other as an appreciative wink to Ethiopian culture.

We were fortunate to have Dinkenesh and Asmara next door. They were well educated to understand what parts of Ethiopian culture might be difficult for us to navigate, yet still firmly rooted in Ethiopian traditions and social norms. Their compound was somewhat unusual for our neighborhood because they were wealthy enough to afford a single-family compound that wasn't shared with other families or individuals. It also had a sturdy wood gate with a lock. Our gate was prone to getting pushed open by passing cows or horses who couldn't resist the untrampled grass inside.

We invited friends and neighbors over to eat with us, but the invitation was usually only accepted once, if ever. They knew we couldn't make food they would like as much as their own. So, I always tried to find other ways to reciprocate people's generosity. This could be having a picture printed, giving them vegetable seeds, or helping them care for their trees. Our neighbors had a beautiful African redwood growing in the front of their compound.

African redwood (*Hagenia abyssinica*), known as *Kosso* in Amharic, is one of Ethiopia's most charismatic trees. It doesn't have any close relatives anywhere in the world. These trees are either male or female. A mature male and female Kosso must be near each other for the female tree to produce seeds. This evolutionary trait maximizes genetic diversity, but much of the tree's natural range in the Simien Mountains has been turned into cropland, grazing land, or eucalyptus plantations. This means that natural seedlings are rare. Most young trees in the mountains have been hand planted from seedlings grown in conservation tree nurseries.

African redwood grows naturally in Ethiopia, Sudan, Kenya, Uganda, Rwanda, Burundi, Tanzania, The Democratic Republic of Congo, Tanzania, Malawi, and Zambia. Despite its wide range throughout the rest of Africa, the tree is now only found in small, isolated areas and is one of Ethiopia's most threatened trees. Its wood is highly valued when cut, but it is usually cut to clear new land for livestock grazing or growing cold-hardy crops—meaning it isn't replanted. African redwood has an interesting adaptation to the harsh high-altitude conditions, where it has been able to maintain a modest foothold. It grows best between 7,500 and 11,000ft (2,300–3,400m) where the atmosphere is thinner and more ultraviolet (UV) radiation reaches the ground. This tree has adapted by making its own sunblock. The subtle, attractive pink hue of the leaves is from molecules that filter radiation, protecting its fleshy leaves from sunburn.

Every part of this unique tree is useful. As its English name suggests, its wood is red and dense—great for furniture and crafts. The wood can be split easily when dried, burns with a pleasant smell, and releases significant heat when burned, making it an excellent firewood. Tool handles made from slightly curved branches are very sturdy and are easy on the hands due to the soft, papery bark. Its showy flowers produce copious nectar and pollen for bees, and its stout branches also make it well-suited for supporting traditional beehives above the reach of thieves and predators.

African redwood's growth during the rainy season is nothing short of astounding. New leaves open and old leaves fall

Derek pruning a Kosso tree.

daily. One tree grew in front of our compound as well. I collected leaves every day and used them as mulch in the garden. The wide, layered canopy was also excellent at slowing torrential rains and allowing water to soak into the soil without it washing away. Some Ethiopian researchers blame the loss of such high leaf-litter producing trees for declines in Ethiopia's agricultural productivity.

However, the tree is best known for its medicinal properties. It's female flowers, and the medicine made from those flowers, all share the same name. The medicinal properties of the tree and the tree itself are inseparable in some people's minds. The tree is medicine. For centuries it has been used to treat tapeworms in both humans and animals. Some anecdotal evidence suggests that even honey derived from the tree's nectar has some deworming potential. Historically, the tree's flowers were an indispensable ingredient of European pharmacies but were gradually replaced with extracts from other plants. African redwood stopped being planted as much when the medicinal export market dried up, and fast-growing eucalyptus trees were planted instead. These relatively recent (1890s) arrivals from Australia not only outcompeted native trees for water, nutrients, and sunlight, they could also completely suppress native tree regrowth as their decomposing leaves release natural herbicides.

The advantages of eucalyptus trees were that they grew fast, required little attention to grow, and regrew from the stump and roots when cut. It could be harvested every ten years. The tree proved successful from the onset. Today, eucalyptus trees are found everywhere in Ethiopia, to the point that many visitors assume that it is native to Africa. Its rapid growth, unpalatability to animals, and well-established market for its wood continue to make it a popular choice to plant in villages and on field edges.

As a forester, trees were central to my work in Ethiopia. I

worked with our compound-mate Misgano to build a small tree nursery in Debark. This unfortunately wasn't successful because the guard we hired rarely showed up and livestock would knock down the fence to nibble the young seedlings. I also taught several classes at the Wondo Genet College of Forestry in southern Ethiopia. However, my favorite activities were teaching younger students about trees and how much we rely on them every day.

Misgano planting a tree seedling

Claire and I co-directed a summer camp for high schoolers called Camp GLOW (Girls Leading Our World). This empowering week-long camp is organized by PCVs around the world. Our camp included male and female campers, but some camps choose to only host girls. Campers learn about personal, environmental, and community health. I made sure to include several activities involving trees.

One of these activities used a "tree cookie," a top-down view of the inside of a tree, as an analogy for important things that happened in each camper's life. The very center of the round tree cookie symbolized the year students were born, and then each ring out from that was a year in their lives. Campers were asked to draw both good and bad things that were important to making them the person they had become. I gave examples like having to move away from someplace they had lived, them or a family member getting sick, or a family member getting a good paying job that provided more comforts and opportunities for education. The result was both much darker and more hopeful than I ever expected. Students listed off personal tragedies as straight-faced as if they were listing books they recently read. Some were orphans living with extended family. Some had watched powerlessly as friends and family died from disease or injury. Some had to walk for hours every day to attend school.

However, there were plenty of good years as well—meeting best friends, someone recovering from illness, or a great harvest that allowed a little extra spending. Trees don't pretend trauma never happened. They cannot replace damaged tissue with new cells. They try to minimize the damage caused by a wound to the fewest number of rings (years) possible and pump defensive compounds into the wood directly around the wound. In many cases, this protective wood is stronger and more resistant to decay or pests than undamaged wood.

This is not to say that it's a good thing for trees to be injured, just as it isn't desirable for people. But being injured is unavoidable. It is the response to that injury—that trauma—that can be beneficial. The word trauma comes from the Greek word for "wound," and many of the young campers were deeply wounded by what they had experienced in their lives. Their trauma often extended for years, through multiple rings and deep into their cores. It wasn't visible from the outside, but each had weathered their own droughts, forest fires, and windstorms. Instead of crumpling, they sank their roots deeper, grew stronger wood, and reached for the sun.

THE VIRTUE OF RAPE

"Throughout history, it has been the inaction of those who could have acted; the indifference of those who should have known better; the silence of the voice of justice when it mattered most; that has made it possible for evil to triumph."
—Haile Selassie I

"The difficulty lies not so much in developing new ideas as in escaping from the old ones."
—John Maynard Keynes

Incense, wood smoke, and stale body odor hung like a curtain over the door as I walked inside. I turned my head and coughed as quietly as I could, not wanting to announce myself as a newcomer. The interior of the *t'ella bet*, a traditional beer house, was lit by a pair of exposed incandescent light bulbs hanging on wires from the ceiling. T'ella, pronounced with a hard T, is a mildly alcoholic drink primarily brewed in the homes of Orthodox Christians as a relaxing and surprisingly nutritious way to spend time with friends.

This homebrew is made by mashing local grains, such as teff and barley, in water steeped with the bitter leaves of buckthorn bushes. The leaves, called *gesho* in Amharic, act as a flavoring much like hops in Western beers. However, the leaves serve a greater purpose than flavoring, which is good because the flavor is terrible. Like the delicate white bloom on wine grapes, the leaves are covered in hardy yeasts that turn the grain sugars into alcohol. The result is an earthy-sweet slurry that is allowed to ferment in sealed jugs for several days. The t'ella, which now has the consistency of runny oatmeal, can be served unfiltered or can be filtered into a slightly less pungent, cleaner pour.

The drink is common at social events and has even been adopted in some religious ceremonies instead of wine. Grapes don't grow well in the highlands, so historically Jews and Christians have substituted t'ella for wine. Wine is now available, but the relatively high cost and low quality make it much less common. T'ella and the homes where it is sold are an acquired taste. Some PCVs and other international workers enjoy the taste and compare it to lambic-style beers made with wild yeasts. Having lost a third of my body weight to dysentery during training, I limited how much questionable liquid I drank. I didn't have any more weight to lose to unruly amoebas.

I had reluctantly accepted a friend's invitation to join him for t'ella while on the way to the market. Yohannes had invited me for a drink numerous times before, but I always declined. The person inviting you to eat or drink together usually pays, so I could not use being short of cash as a reason for not going. I had run out of excuses and did genuinely want to grab a drink with a friend. This was just like going to a bar in the USA. Though, in this case, the bar was in someone's two room house, only served one drink, and that drink tasted like it was strained with moldy bread and served out of a shoe. We carefully made our way to a narrow rawhide bench on the far wall of the room as our eyes adjusted from the bright sun outside. I almost tripped over the staff of a man on the way. The man stared at me passively as I apologized for not seeing him in the dim light. He accepted my apology with an indifferent nod and reached for a cup of t'ella on a small pink table to his right. His lack of interest was refreshing—I was just a white guy speaking Amharic—in a town with only three white people. It felt good to not stand out. The man's traditional cow horn cup looked both comically out of place and in perfect harmony on top of what was obviously a kiddie table with fake fluorescent roses running down its legs. In a land of generational poverty, gaudiness is next to godliness.

The man took a generous sip and returned the cup to its Pepto Bismol pink resting place. I took a closer look at the man as I sat down next to Yohannes. He was older than I originally thought. The deep lines of his face were hidden by dark skin, unusually dark for an Ethiopian—the result of a lifetime outside in high altitude sun. His skeletal hands and face, the only body parts left uncovered, would have been indiscernible in the dark were it not for his customary creamy-white clothing. His *gabi* flowed over his narrow shoulders and was loosely folded behind his head to form a hood. This hood, normally used to protect against harsh weather, now acted as a neck pillow. His Gordian knot of a turban, twisted tightly around his head, set him apart as an Orthodox priest.

Having realized this, I took a closer look at his staff. The long wooden handle was hand carved and topped by a broad piece of brass shaped like an uppercase T. Called *maq-wam-iya* in Amharic, the name of these prayer staffs is almost too fun to say to take seriously. Yet they are an important piece of priestly attire. They are walking sticks, processional batons, and percussion instruments. However, they are crucial as crutches to support priests under the armpit, allowing them to stand for hours-long liturgies in ancient *Ge'ez*. The wood and metalwork weren't crude necessarily, but they were simple and polished by years of use. He was not from town. His faith existed where recovery from illness is a legitimate miracle and where priests are the most literate members of the community. The word of God and food aid delivered on the back of a donkey keep people alive.

His was an old religion, one of the oldest still observed by a large population. Ethiopia is believed to be the second country to officially adopt Christianity, only after Armenia, and the first in Africa by far. Like Roman Emperor Constantine, King Ezana of the Axumite Empire recognized the political value of forsaking his pagan faith for rising Christian influences—cementing trade ties with Christian Greeks. The first coins minted in Ethiopia were actually written in Greek and measured in fractions of the dominant Roman coinage.

The Ethiopian Orthodox Church is also called The Ethiopian Orthodox Tewahedo Church. *Tewahedo*, meaning "united as one" in Ge'ez, refers to an abstract interpretation of God's nature that ironically separates it from most other Christian denominations. The Church insists that Ethiopia wasn't just one of the earliest adopters of this brand of Christianity, but that the country was religiously significant centuries before. The Arc of the Covenant, containing the original ten commandments, is kept in the closely guarded Chapel of the Tablet in Axum. It was taken there by Menelik I, the first Ethiopian emperor, beloved bastard son of King Solomon, and heir of the Queen of Sheba. Balthazar, one of the three magi that visited Christ in Bethlehem, was actually King Bazen of Axum who ruled during that time. The true cross on which Christ was crucified is buried under a small mountaintop church in Amhara. Are these claims, stated as fact, historically true? It doesn't matter in the slightest. The Orthodox Church is an inseparable part of Ethiopian culture regardless of one's personal religious beliefs.

Yohannes and I sat and drank, listening to the small talk that passed around the room. The t'ella bet was more subdued than usual because the four men that made up the largest group in the room had just come from a session of chewing narcotic *chat* next door. These plant leaves, containing a powerful

Derek standing next to the stele above King Bazen's tomb in Axum.

stimulant, are chewed for hours to produce a cerebral high that ends in a low-energy crash comparable to coming down after drinking a bathtub of black coffee.

The higher paying jobs in Debark are dominated by tourism service providers, such as guides that can speak foreign languages. Less educated people are employed by the Ecotourism Associations which operate as unions of service-specific workers such as pack mule handlers or cooks. Despite the number of tourism-related jobs, there are still hundreds of unemployed people living in Debark. This number swells significantly during the rainy season when tourist numbers plummet, leaving groups of unemployed young men with copious amounts of free time and few responsibilities.

The priest said something disapproving of the young men lounging in their stupor. In Ethiopia, chat is pronounced like it is spelled, however, it is often spelled khat and pronounced like "cat" in Arabic-speaking countries. It is more common among Muslim populations and looked down upon by some older Christians. I didn't understand how the conversation started, but the men took offense to the priest's opinion. They were Christian and saw nothing wrong with occasional use of the drug. One commented that he would chew chat more if it wasn't for the bitter taste and the feeling it left in his mouth. Friction grew between the rural priest and the young townies until the group decided to recuperate somewhere else. They thanked the owner and stood lethargically. The men pushed past the curtain at the front door and stepped out into the bright sun, dramatically covering their eyes.

What the room had lost in occupants, it gained in tension. The departures left only the priest, Yohannes, me, an elderly man, a young man by his side, and a quiet middle-aged man by himself. No one spoke or even moved to lift their cup.

The elderly man across the room broke the silence in support of the priest, "Chat is not for Christians. It is forbidden."

I had only heard *ayfekadum,* the Amharic word for forbidden, used to scold park visitors or in reference to religious law. Chat isn't actually forbidden by the Church, but it is considered distasteful.

The young man to the left of the elder waited for Yohannes to look at him, then opened his eyes wide at him, the Ethiopian equivalent of an eye-roll. The bench Yohannes and I shared bounced lightly from his stifled chuckle. They knew this guy and were used to putting up with him, but they respected him enough not to question him, or knew it would not be productive.

The man sitting by himself did not. "No, it's not," he chided, "Christians can chew chat, like you can drink t'ella. It is not a problem."

Yohannes shifted his weight.

The young man across the room stared forward, now trying to avoid eye contact.

The old man scrunched his brow in disbelief.

The priest took a sip.

The middle-aged man spoke again, louder this time, "Does it say in the Holy Book that Christians cannot enjoy chat?" The man was half-heartedly trying to be polite, but this was obviously a sore subject for him. Based on his outfit, he was likely Orthodox and, based on his response, likely chewed chat himself.

The Ethiopian Orthodox Bible is complex and has more books than any other Christian bible, so it was entirely possible it did say something specifically about chat. However, instead of replying with a relevant chapter and verse, the priest took a broader approach.

The history of the Orthodox Church in Ethiopia is deep and visceral. It saturates the linings of everyday life like incense smoke, both literally and figuratively. Clothing, art, feast days, fasting days, celebration, and mourning all bear the sights, sounds, and smells of Orthodoxy. This dominance comes at a cost for the two-thirds of Ethiopians who identify as Christian, but also those who do not. Most of the remaining third of Ethiopians are Muslim, but there are small groups that still practice traditional (pagan) religions. The cost of religious supremacy is the imprisonment and murder of people in same-sex relationships to protect the country's cultural purity. It is the forced marriage of young girls to older men to protect the girls' purity. It is the restrictive holy days that make poor Ethiopians unable to compete for inflated food prices to, you may have guessed, protect their purity. To quote Voltaire, "God created sex. Priests created marriage."

The brilliance and compassion of Christ's life are demoted into a backstory for the divine tragedy of his death. That is, the radical service of Christ's life is overshadowed by the suffering at its end. This shifting focus from life to death largely took place during the first four centuries following the execution of the historical Christ. Politicking and power struggles within a growing religious class replaced the importance of the *Sermon on the Mount* with religious obligations and conditional "unconditional" salvation. The Ethiopian Orthodox Church is not alone in this religious rewriting but that does not make it less responsible for its outcomes. How would the pending argument with a buzzed priest have been different if the Church had focused on Jesus' life rather than his death?

My growing Amharic vocabulary for navigating Ethiopian bureaucracy and occasional interpretations from Yohannes allowed me to follow the priest's points surprisingly well. Yohannes didn't

The ceiling and walls of Debre Birhan Selassie Church in Gondar completely covered with paintings of biblical stories.

whisper because the priest didn't speak English and freely explained specific phrases he thought were necessary for me to understand. The priest told the man that chat may not be forbidden by the government, but that it took too much focus away from God, meaning that it is forbidden by the Church. He said Christians must prioritize God and live pure lives. If he had stopped there, I could have respected his theological reasoning for a prohibition on recreational drugs. However, the priest didn't stop.

He launched into a spontaneous, but sluggish, sermon on the moral decline of Ethiopian culture and how it reflects poorly on the Orthodox Church, which WAS Ethiopian culture. Our neighbor, who worked in the local social services office, had recently told us about a marriage being planned between a 12-year-old girl and a much older man in a rural area bordering the national park. Such marriages are illegal in Ethiopia but still alarmingly common in religiously conservative, rural communities. Government offices lack the reach and interest to enforce such laws in these communities—unless they risk reflecting poorly on local officials. The wedding was called off just days before it was scheduled to happen. The prepubescent bride-to-be was safe for now, but conditions were still ripe for future arranged marriages of preteen brides to men more than double their age. This priest was one of those conditions.

The laws of God, the priest declared, were more important than any laws men came up with. Whether from age or conviction, the priest's voice shook as he recounted the state government using its secular authority to undo his efforts to ensure the girl was married with her virginity intact. The intended groom had expressed his infatuation with the girl and was unable to control his feelings for her. The priest stepped in to prevent them from sinning by orchestrating the marriage. He was only doing his job to save their souls.

International experiences have helped me temper the inevitable ethnocentrism that comes from comparing one's culture with others. Although, nothing had prepared me to come face-to-face with a respected elder promoting statutory rape as a surefire way to prevent sex before marriage. This is not only a violation of human rights and dignity, but also puts young girls at severe risk for life-threatening medical complications such as internal bleeding, infections, fistulas, and mental illness. *Cutting for Stone*, the bestselling novel by Abraham Verghese, is set in Ethiopia and describes some of these issues in devastating detail.

My teeth clenched and the sour feeling in my stomach grew beyond the effects from the second glass of t'ella I had just finished. My right leg was pumping up and down like those of the girls repairing clothes on the treadle sewing machines we could hear squeaking outside. Yohannes sensed the obvious change in mood and had stopped adding English commentary, unsure how to handle an irate foreign friend that looked ready to punch a geriatric, holy man. PCVs are required to develop a strong tolerance for host country traditions and conflicting views of what we may consider common sense. However, questioning the merits of church-sponsored rape wasn't covered in our culture and language classes. Blaise Pascal, the 17th century French physicist, theologian, and poster child for moderate alcohol drinking has been credited with saying, "Men never do evil so completely and cheerfully as when they do it from a religious conviction." *This priest does evil*, I concluded.

Thankfully, I wasn't the only person who thought so. Despite centuries of war, or maybe because of that history, Amharans value keeping the peace in social situations. They smile. Boats aren't rocked. Apple carts aren't upset. Pots aren't stirred. That is, unless there is a damn good reason. The man who had prodded the priest on chewing chat had found his reason. He stood and took a step forward, glaring red-hot hate at the priest. The priest's expression had not changed the entire time we were in the room together, but now a mix of mild surprise and concern crept up his face, starting at his chin and ending high up his forehead. The man took another step and opened fire with a rattle of Amharic that was too fast and continuous for me to even differentiate words. The priest was more than 10ft away from the yelling man, but he flinched as if struck.

I had no idea what the man said, and Yohannes did not volunteer an interpretation, but everyone sat in shock as the man continued to unload on the priest. I had never seen an Ethiopian lose their temper this way in public before. T'ella may have loosened his tongue, but this was more than lowered social inhibitions. This was contempt. I had admired the man's willingness to question the priest on the virtues of child marriage, but even I was alarmed when he stepped across the room, grabbed the priest's cup, and spat into it. He had grabbed the cup with his left hand, emphasizing the insult. The man contained his anger enough not to strike the priest who stared back at him in total confusion and panic. An older woman, the owner of the t'ella bet, reappeared with a "fresh" jar from the shared bedroom that also functioned as a storeroom. She began shouting at the man, enthusiastically using her free arm to motion him out the door. He shuffled sideways toward the door as he flung up his arms in equal parts anger, embarrassment, and acceptance. The man left without saying another word to the priest, or even looking him in the eye.

Yohannes had finished his third cup, and I certainly didn't need any more to drink. We did not want people to think we were with the yelling man, so we waited for a few minutes after he left before we paid our bill and exited. The priest and his young assistant hadn't said a word since the man began yelling. The owner replaced the cup that was spit into, and the priest made a show of taking an appreciative sip but didn't drink again. I like to think of the priest still sitting there, blankly staring at the extravagantly photoshopped mural of wild animals on the wall of the brewhouse and recalculating his religious arithmetic. However, he likely never questioned his position on marrying off children, just as he likely never questioned why a toucan was sitting in a crabapple tree above a pixelated giraffe. But I do hope, for at least a few minutes, he had the fear of God in him.

PINKIES UP

"Work. Good, honest work, whether it's working with your hands to create an artwork, or manual labour, brings forth a sense of divinity at play. The only prerequisite is that whatever the work is, it is done sincerely and in congruence with the soul's true origin and intent, then, without any effort, one experiences a flow, wherein one feels a part of the plan of the entire universe."
—Kamand Kojouri

"Attention is the rarest and purest form of generosity."
—Simone Weil

Our good friend Negash owned a small café near our home. It was on the corner of the main road and a small side street that led to our compound. Its comfortable vinyl-upholstered chairs would have fit perfectly in a 1980s Mexican restaurant. The setting was simple and traditional. Ornately woven serving trays and handmade tapestries hung on the walls instead of the questionably photoshopped posters that were common in most cafes. We raised money for Negash and our compound-mate Misgano to purchase a basic computer together, which sat on a table in the corner of the café next to a small rack of clothes for sale.

Negash was trying to diversify his income by renting out the computer and selling women's clothes as gifts to his occasionally drunk customers. It was an odd business model, but it successfully allowed him to weather the ups and downs of seasonal income. By covering most of the computer cost, we had unintentionally allowed Negash to charge less for people to use the computer. He only needed to pay for electricity and the USB modem that connected to Ethiopia's cell phone network for internet. This didn't win us any goodwill with the two-computer "internet café" down the road, but it did grant us endless cups of tea in Negash's café.

This small room in front of Negash's house was a safe harbor. It allowed us to leave our compound, even when we didn't have the energy to go to the market or one of our project sites. We could spend hours chatting in a playful mix of Amharic and English, or we could sit silently together, just enjoying each other's company. Whatever dog happened to follow us inside would not only be tolerated but welcomed. Negash also made the best *ambasha* in town, a subtlety sweet round loaf of bread cut into slices like a pie. He ignored traditional gender roles and cooked because he enjoyed it. He worked hard to keep his simple storefront clean and inviting. He didn't advertise to tourists making their way into the national park, but many found their way there because he had a reputation for fair prices—one of the reasons we turned from regular customers to great friends.

Negash was almost always working, but like many younger Ethiopians, he looked down on manual labor. He didn't mind cooking or cleaning, and he was very handy when he needed to be. But he wouldn't dig ditches, till fields, or make furniture. His hands were smooth and his fingernails were kept clean and even. His pinky nails were manicured to inch-long points to announce that he was more than a laborer. He made a living with his mind and his relationships. In Ethiopia, sedentary is luxury. To be called *wolfram*, fat, was a compliment because it meant you could do more than sustain yourself. Increased rates of diabetes and heart disease were shifting this belief in more urban areas, but chubbiness was still desirable in rural Ethiopia.

Artificially distressed clothes, like jeans with torn knees and sweaters with loose threads may be fashionable in developed countries; Ethiopia is the opposite. Those that can afford new clothes make sure they look new. Fashion is either the brilliant-white, flowing fabrics embellished with intricate threadwork traditionally worn for special occasions, or sharp clothes from fast-fashion factories in China. Most rural Ethiopians cannot afford new clothes or avoid calloused hands. More than three quarters of Ethiopians still farm. There are traffic jams caused by uncooperative cattle even in the sprawling capital of Addis Ababa. Ethiopians are not naïve about where food comes from and how much work it takes to produce it, however, they are quick to distance themselves from it—if they can afford to.

We often stopped by Negash's café when returning from trips away from town. There was always hot tea ready, or good

A simple loom outside a weaver's house for traditional Ethiopian clothing.

coffee if we were willing to wait while the beans were pounded into powder and allowed to brew on the charcoal fire. Green (unroasted) coffee is ranked into three broad levels of quality. The first grade is high quality, full beans with no rocks or vegetable matter. The second is medium quality, with beans that are likely smaller or deformed, and there may be some contamination. The third level of quality is almost not even worth drinking. It can have almost as many small rocks or dried leaves as it does actual coffee beans. The lowest quality beans are purchased very cheaply by the rural poor. Most Ethiopians drink the middle grade because that is most widely available. Nearly all the higher quality beans are exported for prices higher than what most Ethiopians can afford. Coffee may have been discovered in Ethiopia, but that still doesn't prevent it from being shipped overseas to the highest bidder.

The coffee in Negash's café was well roasted, strong, and slightly oily from the high-quality beans. However, the best way to wash the road dust out of our mouths was usually a cold beer. Negash didn't have a refrigerator to keep them cool, but there was always a shoe-shine boy nearby who would run a beer over from a restaurant for a few cents and then go collect the deposit for returning the empty bottle.

On one of our trips, we took an opportunity to attend a high-level government meeting in southern Ethiopia. It was held in the lakeside town of Hawassa, at a resort founded by long-distance runner Haile Gebreselassie, Ethiopia's most famous athlete. The resort rests on the shore of Lake Awassa, one of

Ethiopia's largest bodies of water. Many attendees wore stylish suits custom made by tailors in Addis Ababa. There were numerous ferenjis at the meeting, but the PCVs stood out with our business casual button-down shirts and long dresses. Most of the foreigners and Ethiopians at the meeting were too urban to grow their pinky nails out, but still sweltered in their formal wear in the heat of the humid lowlands.

    The few Volunteers attending the meeting were both giddy and disgusted by the lunch catered by the resort. Flawless fruits and vegetables shuttled in from Chinese-owned greenhouses near Addis were used as garnish around the meticulously choreographed main meal. The fruits and vegetables we could get in the highlands were usually overripe and badly bruised by the time they made it to market. The small but productive garden we tended in our own compound supplemented what we could find at market. We never missed an opportunity for fresh

Derek harvesting fresh lettuce from the garden.

vegetables. I caused a few confused looks when I took a whole, raw broccoli head the size of my fist from an artful arrangement on the buffet line.

The resort grounds were beautiful and wouldn't have been out of place on a Caribbean Island. However, the illusion disappeared as soon as you stepped foot off the resort. Fishermen roasting whole fish over charcoal braziers lined the rocky lake shore. Groups of women were beating soap bubbles out of their laundry on submerged boulders. They were topless, and their skirts were rolled up at the waist to keep them dry, or at least drier. Nudity wasn't inherently immodest in the Christian and Muslim communities of the highlands—as long as it was practical. However, such large public displays of skin would never have happened. The southern regions are viewed by some Ethiopians as godless and immoral. This is not helped by the reputation of Shashamane Town, home to Rastafarians who were originally granted land by Emperor Haile Selassie (born Ras Tafari Makonnen). Shashamane sits at a major crossroad just north of Hawassa and while its Rastafarian population has dwindled, its bad reputation remains.

Some fishermen were crossing Lake Awassa in crude canoes, their boats riding so low in the water it looked as if the men were sitting on the water itself, floating cross-legged like exhausted gurus. Their life was hard. Their only days off were on religious holidays—frequent as they were. The skin on their arms shone like burnished leather, and their faces were so dark they looked featureless from shore. Unlike many other lakes I had visited in Ethiopia, Awassa lacked an Orthodox monastery perched on an island in the middle. The fishermen, lost pilgrims, drifted back and forth to reel in their fishing lines and nets. Part of me envied them. But all of me knew I couldn't do their work for a week, let alone an entire lifetime. To them, it wasn't a choice, it was survival. If they wanted to eat, they needed to fish. They didn't have the luxury of long pinky nails. They never took a sick day, unless of course their illness physically prevented them from working. Some were likely combating malaria, some would likely even die from it.

The mosquito is the deadliest animal in all of human history. Its ability to spread disease has killed millions of people and crippled millions more. Peace Corps requires Volunteers to take malaria prophylaxis (preventative medication) in countries with the disease. However, living in the highlands, we saved our meds and only took them when we traveled in the lowlands. The medication's side effects were so unpleasant that we would only take them when absolutely necessary. This would have been justifiable grounds for a forced flight back to the USA if the Peace Corps headquarters found out. Malaria is a debilitating disease and much easier to prevent than to treat. However, hallucinations, nausea, insomnia, and exceptionally vivid nightmares were the cost of protecting oneself from the single-celled parasites mosquitoes carried. Despite not taking the pills most of the time, we were fortunate to have access to them. Some health program Volunteers spent most of their time on malaria education and prevention projects such as bed net distributions and testing.

We were urged not to swim or get anywhere close to the lake water due to the high probability of being infected with another very unpleasant parasitic disease called *schistosomiasis*. This was yet another disease we would be screened for when leaving Ethiopia and given medication for if needed. Volunteers knew it would be taken care of if contracted. Some Volunteers loved eating *kitfo*, raw ground beef with spices and butter. This brought its own obvious health risks, but ones that could be medicated into submission—for anyone with access to a well-stocked pharmacy.

A third of Ethiopians are estimated to be infected with *Ascaris lumbricoides*, a parasitic intestinal roundworm, and a quarter of Ethiopians infected with *Trichuris trichiura*, an intestinal whipworm. Roundworm, tapeworm, whipworm, hookworm...one worm, two worm, red worm, blue worm, many with the potential to cause chronic health issues, or death. However, there is no paid time off for being sick. Volunteers, who may lack the family and community support that Ethiopians have when ill, at least have access to almost any medication if required.

We returned from the meeting in Hawassa sun-kissed and well-fed, but also jaded about how much money had been spent on the meeting. A single lunch was more than a rural family spent on food in a month. I was grateful for the chance to visit a new part of the country, see several friends living in the region, and eat food prepared by professional chefs. Most PCVs live and work apart from these conspicuously well-funded, back-patting parties. Many proudly distance themselves from missionaries, embassy staff, and other foreigners that "slum-it" with daily hot showers, imported breakfast cereal, and assigned chauffeurs. These people aren't somehow bad for having more comfortable life arrangements, but they are often out of touch with the realities of life outside their razor wire-topped compounds.

Too often, well-meaning development workers or foreign service staff are dropped like paratroopers into a country with metaphoric guns drawn, ready to open fire on the first noble cause they see. Instead of asking, "What do you need?" they announce, "This is what you need, and I am here to give it to you." There can be a strong sense of *noblesse oblige* among people engaged in international development projects—the originally French concept that privileged people must act with generosity and nobility toward those less privileged. To put it more plainly in English, "they act like their shit don't stink," and they must teach other people how to live better. This noble ethnocentrism can bring about positive change, but it is change demanded by those doing the work. *Oblige*, in French or English, comes from the Latin word meaning "to bind together." Many people working on development projects abroad ignore this definition. We are tied to the people we are working with. We are not above, we are beside.

The multi-day bus rides from Hawassa to Addis Ababa, Addis to Gondar, and Gondar to Debark left us exhausted when we finally arrived back in town. The trip from Gondar to Debark was especially tiring because a wad of clothing wrapped in a loose shawl in the overhead luggage rack continuously dropped louse larva on the passengers below. Eventually, the bus doorman picked up the offending clothes with two passengers' canes like giant chopsticks and tossed the bundle out the bus door. The owners of both the canes and the infested clothes knew better than to argue with the doorman. Claire and I asked to get off the bus before reaching the dirt lot near the market that functioned as the Debark bus station. We wanted to avoid the "gumboys" who hovered around the buses once they parked. All the boys knew us, and we would be expected to make up for the days we were gone and unable to buy from them. That could wait for the next day once we rested and went to the market to buy food.

We lumbered behind the small storefronts on the main road, along a sparsely traveled, rocky path. The mournful yodel of one of the neighborhood street dogs met us as we ducked into our compound. Without slowing, I threw him a few pieces of the roasted barley we had for a snack on the bus. Thankfully, our hut's door swung outward, otherwise I would have fallen through it from exhaustion once I opened it. We fell onto our short bed, not caring how grimy we were, as a small cloud of dust poofed up around us. We stared at the ceiling for a solid half hour before regaining the energy to even speak to each other.

There wasn't anything to eat at our house because we were away for almost a week and had used up anything perishable before we left. We brought our backpacks in from where we had dropped them out front and poured water from a storage bucket into the top of our water filter to start it trickling through. We knew where we were going next. I bolted the lock on our door, and we walked back toward the main road.

We made it to Negash's café and took our usual seats on a long bench along the front wall. From here we could keep any dogs that followed us away from other customers and avoid people staring at us through the open doorway. One of Negash's buddies was using the computer and greeted us casually as we sat. His relaxed welcome was very appreciated. Our trip left us not wanting to stand out like a sore thumb...or white people in rural Africa. The normalcy of someone not making a big deal about us being in the room was exactly what we needed. He shouted toward the door in the back of the café without taking his eyes off the computer screen. Negash called back that he would be there in a minute.

Our friend soon appeared with a tray of shot glasses overflowing with hot tea. Negash's buddy had shouted there were customers but hadn't specified who, and he winked at us as a surprised Negash called our names. We stood to greet him as he put the tea on our table. Negash shook my hand and pivoted to knock his right shoulder against mine. This "shoulder bump" is usually done three times and ends in a lingering hug. I was admittedly proud to have worked from a single handshake to this traditional greeting among good friends.

At the end of our Peace Corps service, Negash was the last friend we had said goodbye to when we left Debark for the

Negash teaching Claire how to make ambasha bread.

last time. That evening, he called crying, saying that he missed us. One of our street dogs had woken him in the middle of the night, yowling and scratching frantically at his door. He let the dog stay on his floor. The dog knew something was different this time. We wouldn't be coming back. Negash had never seen a dog behave that way, and it broke a part of his kind heart which he never knew could break.

Negash earned his long pinky nails, and I earned the calluses on my hands. One shouldn't be valued more than the other. Ethiopia needs the efforts of engineers, accountants, and bookish, small business owners as much as it needs the efforts of farmers, tree planters, and field biologists. Negash had more skill and kindness in his flamboyant pinky than I had in my whole body.

SMILING WITH DEATH

*"Grieving is an expression of gratitude,
and that expression doesn't have to be rushed."*
—Carolyn Wells

"Those who are afraid of death will carry it on their shoulders."
—Federico García Lorca

Many experiences in Ethiopia didn't seem particularly important or strange until years later, once removed from the realities of daily life there. Ethiopia is a land of dichotomies; or it is at least to a Western observer. What may seem like contrasting situations or ideas are just points on the spectrum of the human condition in the developing world. If F. Scott Fitzgerald is correct that, "The test of a first-rate intelligence is the ability to hold two opposed ideas in the mind at the same time, and still retain the ability to function," then Ethiopians are savants.

Death is ubiquitous and palpable in rural Ethiopia. There was not a day that went by that I did not see, hear, or especially smell signs of death. There is the cowhide bench turned into a litter to carry a family member's body down the town's main street and into the cemetery. There are the wails of grieving parents during their son's *lukso* in the compound next door. There is the olfactory assault from a cat carcass rotting in a shallow puddle at the side of the road. I used to think of death as something acute; something that swooped down and ended life. After living in Ethiopia, I started to think of death as simply something that strolls the streets and leisurely ends lives.

A lukso is a prolonged funeral service that can last for days. Friends and family members gather to mourn, support each other, and pay respect to the deceased. The lukso is never static. There are people constantly coming and going. The atmosphere fluctuates between that of a Holiday feast and of a sinking ship where everyone knows they are going to die sooner than later. They are often very public events. Due to their frequency and longevity, it is difficult not to notice them. I was walking home from the market one day and passed by a lukso being held just outside a t'ella bet.

The wake must have been going on for several days because there were few mourners left, and two huge, plastic jugs of t'ella sat uncapped and empty next to the bench they were on. The participants were in a semicircle, talking, laughing, and passing a picture among themselves. The picture must have been of the recently departed because people would start crying as soon as their fingertips touched the photo frame. The person holding the portrait would sob and rock precariously on the narrow bench as the people on either side moaned and consoled the person charged with holding the image of the newly deceased. They were laughing and smiling one minute and then bleating like whipped cattle the moment they were handed the mourning baton. It seemed disingenuous and narcissistic. I was deeply disturbed by the experience until I realized that despite the highly ritualized process and exaggerated crying, the sorrow was very real. I was seeing a mother weep for her son who had died during a surgery intended to save his life. There was nothing fake about her pain. My initial criticism made me feel awful.

The grief was always there, molten and red, building in their chests. It was only allowed to bubble up and be released once they were handed the picture. It was still a show; a ritual that they had performed countless times before, but it was real, nonetheless. I was ashamed for questioning their pain, but the experience forced me to question the nature of death again since coming to Africa. I no longer thought of death as a *doriye*, a wandering thug who ends lives indiscriminately and dispassionately. Death became a veil that cloaked the town from end to end; listlessly fluttering as the winds from events below moved it up and down. When an event became too significant, the veil would passively settle down to earth, ending lives.

As the picture frame was passed around the lukso, the veil dipped like a tarp filled with rain during a storm, perched inches above the mourners' heads. It was neither malicious nor compassionate. Death could not be dissuaded once its weight settled, and its work could not be undone after it lifted. Death

Funeral Wake in Tigray. Photo by Rod Waddington, Flickr.

stopped being an antagonist that could be prayed away. It was woven by the same hand that crafted the lives that set it waving. It existed for a reason.

I have always believed in the functionality and necessity of dying and the holistic cycling of life, but I had never seen it played out on such a large scale. The veil of death is more common attire in Africa than it is in many other parts of the world, but is still fashionable everywhere. I suppose that because it hangs so much lower in Africa, it is easier to see its design without being smothered by it. Even when faced with death and hardship, many Ethiopians continue to smile. To be afraid whenever death is close here would mean living in constant fear.

"Death smiles at us all; all a man can do is smile back..." has become a cliché used in action movies by the brooding protagonist that claims to not fear death. The movie *Gladiator* attributes this phrase to the stoic Roman Emperor Marcus Aurelius. The phrase is meant as an insult by the fictional gladiator Maximus against Emperor Commodus, who killed his own father in the film. This line of dialogue has led to countless memes and motivational images crediting Marcus Aurelius with the phrase. While apocryphal, to be fair, it still captures the philosophizing emperor's views on mortality. A translated quote from Aurelius' actual writings in his *Meditations* is, "Death hangs over you. While you live, while it is in your power, be good." Death is not met with a smile, because it is neither good nor bad. Death is inevitable. The point of life is not to mock or welcome death, but rather to be a good person before it comes.

The image of Africans smiling with perfect, glowing teeth amid abject poverty has become a powerful image in developed countries, as well as in Africa itself. People may be compelled to give money to stoic, stone-faced individuals surviving against all odds in awful conditions; however, the "Smiling African" is a much more powerful motivator. I believe this is one reason why Ethiopia is such a popular beneficiary for foreign aid. Are there other countries that could make better use of the aid? *Yes.* Based on how the funds are used and their long-term benefits, are there other countries that deserve the aid more than Ethiopia? *Yes.* Are there other countries whose inhabitants can be counted on to smile for a foreigner even when dangerously malnourished, dangerously lacking in basic personal freedoms, or even dangerously hostile to the foreigner? *No.* At least no other countries I have visited.

I cannot count the times I saw tourists fawning over smiling Ethiopian children as they were getting charged five times the usual price for a stick of gum they didn't even want. Nor can I count the times I asked a local government official to do an integral part of their job, but only receiving a smile in return. I cannot recall how many times someone had either successfully or unsuccessfully stolen from me, and for my resentment to have been met by smiling and laughing bystanders. Some smiles, no doubt, are a response to uncomfortable situations. Most are not intended to be malicious, but they often do come across that way.

I had my own mental gallery of pictures from the "Smiling African" collection before I set foot in Africa, and it only increased in size while living there. Here is the "Group of Children Smiling While Playing Football With a Handsewn Ball." This is the uplifting "Students Smiling Shyly While Reading in Their New Library." Here you can see "Mother Smiling While Recounting the Deaths of Her First Three Children." Over here we have the "Starving Mother Smiling While Her Toddler Chews on a Condom Picked Off the Street." Let's not forget "Priest Smiling While Beating a Dog," reminiscent of a dynamic Renaissance painting, or "Minibus Doormen Smiling While Arguing Over Which Van Should Leave First." This is only a fraction of the entire exhibit, but it hopefully provides an understanding of the genre and its diversity.

The ability to smile in the face of poverty, oppression, and even death can be beneficial if not essential for survival. Even for a foreigner, a smile can mean getting a project approved, making a much-needed friend, or the simple affirmation that you can still be happy. Studies have revealed the importance of smiles in leading a happy and fulfilling life. The psychophysiological feedback between your facial muscles and your brain can make you happier than the thing you were originally happy about. It is a feedback loop of positivity. Your smiling face tells the brain behind it to be happy, and so you become happier merely from smiling. Is this why Ethiopians smile so easily and inexplicably? Have they learned to kick-start their brain's happiness?

However, instead of adding to feelings of contentment, a counterfeit smile can drain one's happiness faster than a clenched fist and a full-bodied frown. The energy spent prodding an unwilling smile is physically minuscule yet mentally exhausting. A genuine smile, on the other hand, a smile that does not result from the very conscious decision to smile, can fill someone with an unquenchable desire to wrap the world up in a blanket, meet its eyes, and coo at its beauty. Unfortunately, such genuine smiles were as rare in Africa as a good bowel movement (the two were probably correlated).

I realized that these genuine smiles were once as abundant as bison on the American Great Plains. In this analogy, I suppose moving to Ethiopia was as damaging to my facial calisthenics as European settlers to the American buffalo. It doesn't really matter if you visualize genuine smiles as bison, giant pandas, or altruistic televangelists; the point is that there are few of them. I was very aware that I romanticized life back in America while away, because it was objectively easier. However, I didn't know how to answer when people asked me what I missed most about living in America. The answer was not TV, a flush toilet, or Colorado microbrews. It was matching a passing, authentic smile with one of my own.

    I was regularly scolded for not smiling in Ethiopia. Ethiopian friends would tell me to *techawot*, "to play" or have a good time with them. This came from a genuine desire for me to be happy and enjoy myself. Although, as someone with a resting face like a perplexed serial killer, this happened more often than was helpful. There were undeniably more positive experiences than bad ones as a Volunteer in rural Africa; yet I still found it difficult to smile around so much relative poverty, difficulty, and death. Instead of romanticizing smiles, I catastrophized them. I thought the easy smiles of passing Ethiopians were mocking death, rebelliously laughing in its face. I realized I was wrong. They were not smiling *at* death, they were smiling *with* death because anything else would be a waste.

PART II

THE WAR ON VEGAN MONKEYS

"People don't get the big picture—animals matter, people matter, and animals in the lives of people matter."
—Noel Fitzpatrick

"The man who kills the animals today is the man who kills the people who get in his way tomorrow."
—Dian Fossey

SMNP was included on the UNESCO List of World Heritage in Danger for most of its existence. It was only removed from this "naughty list" in 2017 after park officials demonstrated consistent commitment to better protect the park's resources. This means very little without first mentioning the unique plants and animals that caused it to be listed as a World Heritage Site to begin with. Ethiopia is one of the 25 most biodiverse countries in the world. Endemism is common in Ethiopia's high mountains; some plants and animals found in the Ethiopian highlands are not found anywhere else on Earth. Their high-elevation habitats are islands that shrink as the climate warms and human settlements expand. If not protected, some species will likely become extinct before they are even identified.

Expeditions to the Simien Mountains in 1958 and 1968 returned extensive collections of plants, but some of the species identified during these trips have not been seen in the mountains since. Meaning, some plants have been lost from the area during the past half-century. Unfortunately, large botanical collections from the area were destroyed in bombings on Berlin during WWII, so it is difficult to determine how vegetation has changed.

Charismatic wildlife and a few highly visible plant species, such as tree heather and the Dr. Seussian-looking Giant Lobelia, guide many management decisions in the mountains. Even if more effort is made to protect lesser-known plants, reliable information is notoriously difficult to gather in Ethiopia. Ethiopian and international projects often provide conflicting data for the same subject and lack common methods that specify how data is collected, who collects it, and when it is collected—all of which impact results.

An example of this difficulty is shown in attempts to estimate the extent of Ethiopia's forests. A 2001 Food and Agriculture Organization (FAO) report estimated the area of Ethiopia's high-elevation forests at around 14 million acres (5.8 million hectares). In 2005, FAO reported that the same forest types covered around 32 million acres (13 million hectares) despite the FAO's predicted annual deforestation rate of about 350,000 acres (142,000 hectares) for that period. Instead of reflecting a loss of over 1.2 million acres (486,000 hectares), the new estimate was more than double the figure reported just four years before. The accuracy of information is improving, but gains are slow. The COVID-19 pandemic and the Tigray War have dealt significant blows to long-term research efforts.

Peace Corps partnered my wife and me with the SMNP office to assist with conservation efforts and agricultural projects to help improve the livelihoods of farmers in or around the park. This partnership was short-lived. Limited park capacity and unrealistic expectations of bringing in large foreign donations quickly caused park staff to lose interest in us. However, before that happened, park staff drove us into the park to visit communities and tourist campsites. The government-issued truck was spartan, but much more comfortable than the back of the Isuzu dump trucks that local residents used to travel through the park. There are three main habitats in the Simien Mountains, and they change as elevation increases: (1) Afromontane forests, (2) Ericaceous belt, and (3) Afroalpine zone. These habitats can be difficult to tell apart due to heavy human use, but I was excited to see all three.

In the truck were Claire and myself, Sisay our park counterpart, Getachew the driver, and a park scout whose name I couldn't understand. The scouts spoke little if any English and were required to accompany visitors in the park. They carried Soviet-era AK-47s to discourage run-ins with *shifta*, bandits. Many scouts, and the shiftas they defend against, were militiamen in their previous lives. These *fano* (volunteer warriors) originally served Emperor Haile Selassie in fighting Italian fascists leading

A park scout prevents tourists from getting too close to the cliff's edge.

up to WWII. However, these militias' glorious beginnings gave way to guerrilla warfare in modern conflicts. Becoming a park scout was the retirement plan for some—if you consider making sure visitors don't fall off cliffs or try to pet monkeys a retirement.

These cliffs drop like a one-sided Grand Canyon, and the hills below flow to the horizon. Debark sits in an area that was once Afromontane (African mountains) forests. The forest was home to endless trees that covered the lower-elevation Simien highlands between roughly 6,200 and 9,800ft above sea level (1,900–2,300m). These forests have become an abstract concept. They were cleared for firewood and cultivation due to high human population in the more hospitable climate of the lowlands. The remaining patches of native trees can hardly be called forests and are dispersed along the base of the volcanic escarpment—on land impossible to cultivate or log. These patches often only cover an area of several 100ft^2 (10m^2).

We passed the park gatehouse at Sawre, a small plateau leading into the mountains. The large stone house where we stayed before moving to Debark sat empty. The guard camp at the park gate was built with foreign funds, and it showed. Impressive masonry work and shiny new, corrugated steel roofing made it stand out next to the cluster of small, traditional mud structures with thatch roofs beside it. The house had two bedrooms and a large open room. It was significantly larger than we needed, but the inside was cold, damp, dim, and home to no less than two dozen rats. It was impossible to sleep without waking to the feeling of one running over the bed, but I could not blame the rats. The stone walls were easy to climb, and the building was a fortress from predators.

A dark patch of recently disturbed soil near the road was distinct against the light, dry grass. A large, wooden hitching post for horses had once stood there. Another PCV from our training group stayed with us in the stone house while his own house was being completed at a new guard camp next to the Limalimo Pass. He had brought a hammock from the USA and had hung it between the wood post and a park sign several paces away. There was not much for him to do until his house was finished, so much of his time was spent reading in the hammock. However, the federal warden responsible for the park was taking a rare trip to one of the campsites when he noticed the hammock and its comfortable occupant. Instead of requesting that the hammock be taken down, the warden ordered the post be completely removed.

Our driver Getachew exchanged pleasantries with the guard who dropped the crude rope that functioned as the main park gate, and we continued into the mountains. The heavily rutted dirt road led us past waterfalls, occasional huts, and near vertical hillsides being plowed by single horses to prepare the soil to grow barley. Plowing these fields was slow and dangerous. Erosion during the rainy season exposed rocks that farmers had to move to the field edges as they appeared.

The soil grew shallower and the air colder as the truck climbed, and we entered the Ericaceous belt. It is named for the tree heather (botanical name *Erica*) which grows in a band of elevation throughout the mountains. The belt used to cover nearly all suitable land from 9,800 to 12,500ft (3,000–3,800m) in elevation. The heather forests in the Simien Mountains are unique because their elevation range doesn't match other mountain sites in eastern Africa. Unfortunately, much of this forest has been cleared for fuel and to cultivate cereal crops. The trees that are left often have a stunted, shrubby shape from people harvesting firewood and livestock nibbling on new growth. The forests are also burned to improve grazing which affects both the way trees grow and kills vulnerable tree seedlings.

The tree heathers were covered in veils of cobweb-like lichens. The lichen hangs below the tree canopies, pulling moisture from the fog that flows between the trees and over the cliffs. The stringy, spongy lichen drips water onto the ground below and releases moisture into the air as midday sun clears the fog. If this happens quickly, the trees appear to be steaming. Researchers in a similar forest in east Africa estimated that these lichens absorb as much as 5,000 gallons per acre (46,800 liters per hectare) every year. Giant St John's Wort often grows with *Erica* trees, but these shrubs are heavily nibbled on by goats and sheep in the park. The stunted, arms-length masses of tight leaves bear little resemblance to their natural shape.

We drove over a narrow ridge with steep drops on either side. The exposure was no worse than a mountain road in Colorado, but the constant swaying of the truck made the road edges feel uncomfortably close. The road dropped down into the first of three main campsites in the park. Sankaber Camp was a cluster of mud and cinder block structures tucked into the remaining trees growing along the cliffside. When asked about the camp name, Sisay said it existed before the camp was developed and could be interpreted as "wooden door." Sankaber was set at a bottleneck along the escarpment, with the road built to follow the established trail that led through the narrow pass—acting as a door opening farther into the mountains.

Sankaber was home to a long-running University of Michigan project to research the Gelada monkeys that grazed the highland plateaus. A rotating team of graduate students and researchers lived in a large cinder block roundhouse on the escarpment's edge for months at a time, chronicling the complex Gelada social groups and activities. When not scribbling transcriptions of Gelada conversations and collecting monkey stool samples, the researchers hosted meals attended by local

Derek having a beer with friends at the Sankaber lookout.

Ethiopians and intrepid trekkers headed for Ras Dejen, Ethiopia's highest mountain. Peace Corps did not want Volunteers to live this far into the park because of concerns about how long it would take to get to the closest airport in Gondar if evacuations were needed. Claire and I spent numerous nights in the researchers' cliffside castle and became lifelong friends with several researchers.

One evening, I tiptoed to the edge of the escarpment and glanced down. Instantly struck by vertigo, I felt the churning tightness in my stomach causing my legs to lock and my eyes to swim. Hills crashed against the base of the cliff thousands of feet below, clusters of circular huts adrift on the barley-brown waves. The tin roofs of these rafts were partially hidden by the green spray of unruly eucalyptus plantations around them. A Gelada researcher set one hand on my shoulder and pushed a cold beer bottle into my grip with the other. That was the first, last, and only time a beer bottle ever made me steadier. There are few experiences more magnificent than savoring an ice-cold Ethiopian lager, a luxury itself, watching the sun set on the Roof of Africa. The sun slowly, almost carefully, climbed down the stepped cliff to the fields a half-mile below.

As poet Gary Snyder wrote, "Nature is not a place to visit, it is home." And if architect George Nakashima is correct (I think he is) in considering a tree to be our most intimate contact with nature, then forests are our home in a way no other kind of wilderness can be. This is especially true in the deforested African highlands. Sankaber became a refuge for us and the monkeys our friends studied.

Gelada "baboons" (*Theropithecus gelada*) are the only species of their genus, meaning they don't have any close relatives. There are fossil records of other species, but they have gone extinct, leaving these primates alone at the family reunion. Calling them baboons is inaccurate because they are more closely related to monkeys than baboons. This is a distinction I didn't appreciate until I was schooled on primate taxonomy by a buzzed graduate student. The researchers defend this distinction because geladas lack the aggression often associated with baboons.

Geladas get their name from the Amharic word for "ugly." Despite their fierce faces and impressively long canine teeth, geladas are herbivores. They spend their days sitting in groups, picking grass and roots with their dexterous fingers. Nights are spent nestled tightly against the cliff side to protect against predators such as leopards, Ethiopian wolves, and humans. They are not endangered, but the population is steadily declining due to its naturally restricted habitat and human encroachment into it. Despite this, the federal government allowed foreign tourists to hunt geladas for 3,000 dollars at the time we lived in Ethiopia. Thankfully, I never heard of a foreign visitor hunting them for sport or even requesting to do so.

Constant complaints about geladas from people living inside the park, and inflated population counts by park staff, likely encouraged the government to allow paid hunts. Exhaustive surveys done by the university researchers showed only 10% of the population numbers given by park staff and the guide association. The Gelada Research Project conducted a census while we were there in 2011, which upset the park staff. There was a clear discrepancy between the actual monkey population and the questionable figures the park based its management actions on.

I personally heard a park guide telling visitors that the geladas were overgrazing the park and that their numbers should be reduced through firing squads. Discussions with researchers, visitors, and locals revealed that while such comments weren't common, they weren't rare either. Conflicts between geladas and humans living inside the park happen daily. These are often the result of monkeys orchestrating surprisingly complex raids on crop fields along their native grazing routes, or from shepherds forcing grazing geladas off pasture so their livestock can graze.

Conflict between people and geladas has been going on for centuries; as long as overworked soil in the lowlands forces more people into the mountains than the area can naturally support. Park Warden C.W. Nicol thought the residents cared only for,

> "Those things that had a direct pragmatic meaning to their life. Like young cattle or new shoots of grain, or land brought under the plow, the ownership of a rifle, the words and teachings of the Church or of the Mosque."

Conversations with park visitors often include comments about the high number of livestock within the park. A common complaint is that herders drive their livestock near or directly into wildlife that tourists are watching. I conducted a visitor satisfaction survey as part of my research on park management. When asked about how well the park office manages the environmental impact of park residents, this was what one visitor wrote, "There are so many herds of livestock and people that visitors cannot enjoy the true splendor of the mountains. Children shouting and throwing stones at geladas." Personally, every opportunity I had to watch large groups of gelada monkeys grazing, a shepherd drove his sheep directly through the band, almost as a game. These lunchtime interruptions disrupt their behavior and frustrate visitors who come to view wildlife.

A Discovery Channel special focusing on the relationship between geladas and people living within the national park aired in 2011. It painted a picture of sharp-toothed hordes of monkeys raiding the barley fields of malnourished mountain children. One child interviewed during the show said that the gelada monkeys frequently kill sheep. Another child said she was afraid that a large gelada would carry her off. Many park residents were convinced that geladas were violent and cunning, sometimes blaming them for the mysterious disappearances or deaths of both livestock and humans. When directly asked if they had witnessed an attack on humans or livestock, park residents replied that they knew of someone else who knew someone who had witnessed a gelada attack.

Of the dozens of people I interviewed in the park, none of them had personally witnessed an attack. A Lonely Planet guidebook for Ethiopia included a brief section on negative attitudes toward gelada monkeys in the Simien Mountains. One extreme case involved a gelada accused of breaking into a man's house, dragging him nearly a mile to a cliff, and throwing him off. Strange or potentially embarrassing instances, such as unwanted pregnancies, have been blamed on the monkeys. One presumably well-trained park guide told me the monkeys should be removed so they don't impregnate and hybridize with the sheep—an insult to God. I assumed he was joking at first, but it was a legitimate fear for him. Despite stories like these, the miniature boogeymen are more often viewed as large vermin instead of something supernatural.

A study sponsored by the Frankfurt Zoological Society looked at crop losses from geladas at multiple sites in and around the park. The study estimated that farming households lost 235–280lbs (107–127kg) of their annual harvest to monkeys. Crops and livestock grew poorly in these rocky, high-elevation fields, and farmers relied on domestic or foreign aid to supplement the

Mother and baby gelada monkeys grazing grass clipped short by sheep.

little they could grow. Any loss in crop value threatened the livelihoods of these subsistence farmers. It was also found that fields located farther from the park boundary, i.e. farther from gelada habitat, received less damage than those fields close to the boundary. The researchers concluded that the losses were not solely the fault of the monkeys themselves, because the crops were almost irresistible to them.

Native grass is the monkey's main food source. Compared to these grasses, cultivated cereal crops often have increased yields and grow rapidly. Their high nutritional value make crop-raids a no-brainer for the monkeys. A possible solution can be to create a gelada sanctuary in which cultivation and livestock grazing are not allowed. Farmers outside this sanctuary can then be compensated for damage from geladas. Alternatively, cultivation zones away from monkey habitats can be designated, in which farmers can be compensated for losses. Either case will require a network for monitoring gelada raids on cereal crops and a reparations system to pay for losses. It has been additionally suggested that crops less vulnerable to gelada raiding should be researched. All these solutions will take a focused effort and additional funding—neither of which is likely to be found.

Our truck stopped at the campsite so we could see, and use, the pit latrines that had been built just a few years before. We got back in the truck after a brief stretch and continued—wanting to get as far into the park as we could before running out of daylight. At this time, we didn't know the researchers yet and were still ignorant of the apparently obvious differences between baboons and monkeys. The trees and grazing gelada thinned as we left Sankaber. I sighed in relief and patted the small bag of *kolo,* a common roasted barley road snack, that I had in my pocket. We had escaped gelada territory with our snacks intact and without anyone getting pregnant.

ONWARD AND UPWARD

*"Nature provides a free lunch,
but only if we control our appetites."*

—William Ruckelshaus

"As you gain elevation [on the mountain] your IQ goes down—but your emotional affect goes up, which is great for having a mythic experience, whether you want to or not."

—Stewart Brand

SMNP is the most visited national park in Ethiopia. Total revenue from visitation fees is more than double that of any other Ethiopian national park in the past quarter century. However, most of this money is sent to the federal government, and a fraction goes back to park management.

The national park is one of the first natural areas in the world to be designated a World Heritage Site. The spectacular landscape and endemic wildlife make it a top priority for environmental protection. The rugged topography and high number of native species are directly related because the landscape has created isolated ecological conditions that have led to a variety of animals and plants. Not only is the area important for wildlife, its ecological services provide economic benefits for Ethiopians and neighboring countries through agriculture and tourism. The value of the park as a protected natural area has conflicted with its use by the human communities that existed there before the park was established. This conflict is common among Ethiopian (un)protected areas.

An environmental crisis is an imbalance between a human population and the natural resources it relies upon. This imbalance reduces and endangers the ability of the environment to meet the needs of the human population it supports. More than 60% of all land in Ethiopia above 9,800ft (3,000m) has been converted into cropland. The degraded park environment caused by the mismanagement of natural resources, compounded by extreme weather, threatens not only the human population but also dozens of plant and animal species. Many are found nowhere else in the world. The word "crisis" comes from a Greek word for "decision" or "turning point." Tough decisions need to be made about the park and what can be done to protect its intrinsic value and its value for people.

Following reports of declining Walia ibex populations in the park, a UN monitoring mission was conducted in 1996. The mission recognized declining Ethiopian wolf and ibex populations with increasing human pressures on the park. Based on its findings, the World Heritage Committee decided to immediately add SMNP to the List of World Heritage in Danger. Another monitoring mission was sent in 2001 because the Amhara state government was insulted by the park's placement on that list. This second report praised the government's efforts to address environmental threats and the improved management of the park. However, the World Heritage Committee decided that park conditions required it stay on the list. As a compromise, four benchmarks were created to guide the removal of SMNP from the List of World Heritage in Danger. Yet again, a follow-up monitoring effort found that none of these benchmarks had been met.

The park boundary was redrawn to encompass important wildlife corridors and habitat, and Ras Dejen Mountain was added to allow visitors to summit it without crossing park boundaries multiple times. These new park boundaries were mapped by multiple foreign agencies including Swiss and Austrian institutions. However, this represented little more than a line on a computer screen for many Ethiopian policymakers. The boundaries had been redrawn to exclude human settlements, but these settlements still relied on park resources, and pushing them off the park map did not stop the illegal use of park lands or their impact on park visitors.

Visitation in the national park can be separated into four seasons in most years: (1) Early high season [September and October], (2) Peak season [November to January], (3) Late high season [February and March], and (4) Low season [April to August]. Visitation closely follows *Kiremt*, the rainy season. The end of the rainy season signals the start of the early high season. Early season visitors to the park are treated to a lush, green landscape, blooming flowers, and spectacular waterfalls. The tradeoff is they are also at a greater risk of poor road and trail conditions, poor visibility, hailstorms, and less wildlife activity. The park is still green through peak season but steadily turns brown as the last rains of the year fall. The weather is cool but dry during peak season, and many package tours visit for winter holidays. Visitation is steady after New Year and gradually decreases until the Ethiopian Epiphany (*Timket*) holiday in late January. The park experiences a small surge in visitors as people travel there after celebrating Timket in nearby Gondar. Visitation drops quickly until April, when only a few hundred people come each month until the beginning of the next early high season.

Our first drive into SMNP was early in the low season—before the spring rains started. The thousand-foot waterfalls were dry between Sankaber and the next camp. The truck kicked up a cloud of dust that traced our winding route upward. A rectangular cinderblock building appeared suddenly as we topped a ridge. I had been staring in awe at the impressive terraces on the steep slopes on either side of the valley we drove up, so the

Ethiopian Orthodox priests blessing a river for the Timket holiday.

building's appearance would not have been as abrupt to someone paying attention to the road. The building was the community-run lodge at the Gich Camp. Each campsite had a lodge that trekkers could stay in if they preferred not to sleep in a tent. These basic lodges provided welcome shelter during rain and the occasional snow, as well as a primitive mattress instead of the rocky ground. The lodges didn't, however, provide any protection from the crisp highland cold because they weren't entirely concrete. Primitive wood shutters instead of glass windows did little to stop the constant breeze from wicking warmth away.

A stack of eucalyptus firewood and several woven plastic bags of charcoal sat under the lodge's wide eaves. Firewood and basic food items were sold to the community lodges that then prepared and sold them to visitors staying at the lodges or the campsites surrounding them. Park visitors could hire cooks who would buy food for treks. For many visitors, the cooks' small price markup on food was worth avoiding the chaos and confusion of Debark's sprawling market.

The scout managing our lodge was expecting us and had already started boiling water for coffee. The lanky, clean-shaven man in army fatigues welcomed us warmly when we entered. He formally invited us to sit on the wooden stools arranged in a circle around the charcoal stove he was tending. Both the stove and percolating clay coffee pot, called *jebena*, are mass produced in Ethiopia and can be found in nearly every home—regardless of wealth, religion, and political affiliation. Coffee is neutral ground, the Ethiopian equivalent of breaking bread. We learned that the scout's name was Dawit and it was his third season in the park. Dawit wrapped a red fleece Hello Kitty blanket over his shoulders as he spoke, making himself comfortable. A stooped young woman silently entered the room and squatted by the stove. She removed the jebena and swapped it out with a shallow aluminum pot in a single, fluid movement. We sat in awkward silence as the soot-scorched pot rattled and began to fill the room with the unmistakable smell of popcorn.

"*Fendisha?*" Claire asked.

Dawit, who had not stopped smiling since we sat down, nodded appreciatively at the Amharic. "*Oww, fendisha. Betam tikus.* Yes, popcorn. Very fresh."

The young woman repositioned her skirt and smiled shyly. I strained my conversational Amharic to ask if the woman was Dawit's wife. He chuckled lightheartedly and responded with a

Traditional jebena on charcoal stove.

short monologue that I lost track of after only a few sentences. I told Dawit I didn't understand and turned to Sisay for clarification. Dawit nodded and stared at the embers in the stove. Sisay explained the woman's name was Zinab, which literally means "rain," and that she was Dawit's "camp wife." Sisay could tell from my silence that I still didn't understand. He paused, clearly unsure how best to approach the question.

"Dawit is from Addi Arkay, a village to the north near the Tigray Region border. He has a family there, a wife and children. His job is here in the park. It can take several days to travel there. He sends money back but cannot visit often. Zinab is his wife in the park. She cooks and washes clothes."

"*Ishee,*" I slowly replied, "OK," still uncertain about the relationship between them.

Sisay relented, his patience well-needed when explaining cultural differences to ferenjis, "She is his wife in the park. They live together."

"So, Dawit has two wives?"

"Yes, Dawit and Zinab have a baby."

"They have a baby?"

"Yes, a boy baby."

"Is Dawit Muslim?"

"No, he is Christian."

"He is Christian and has two wives...two families?"

"Yes, it is cultural. It is cultural. The husband does not cook or clean, but he has a job and takes care of family. He does not know how to do these things."

Dawit was watching our exchange with interest but didn't know enough English to follow. Sisay gave her a brief explanation of the conversation, to which Dawit smiled, equally proud and uncertain about what we thought of this arrangement. We finished our obligatory three cups of coffee, ate a polite amount of popcorn, and thanked Dawit and Zinab. As we left the unlit lodge, the brightness outside made us squint. When my eyes adjusted, I was confused at what I saw. A pair of unoccupied tents were the only sign of human activity on the field outside the lodge when we initially arrived. But now, a crowd of a dozen children had gathered near our truck. Getachew, the driver, had stayed with the truck and was half-engaged in conversation. When someone noticed we had reappeared outside, the entire group leisurely moved toward us, three children in front. Their steps hurried as they got closer. Claire and I eyed each other, Sisay looked more annoyed than alarmed. We would get very used to this type of mob greeting by the end of our time in Ethiopia, but it was disarming this early in our service. The children excitedly ran the last ten feet to us and enthusiastically waved crafts in our faces—colorful baskets woven from grasses and plastic bags, musical instruments made from plastic water bottles, and whips made from cords of frayed nylon.

Derek interviewing children in the Simien Mountains about the crafts they make and sell.

Crafts can be an important piece of culture-based tourism because they reflect particular people at a particular point in time. They are pieces of history that you can hold and feel the weight of. They can even tell stories that the people who made them often can no longer tell. However, the value of traditional Ethiopian crafts for park visitors has been overlooked by tourism service providers and local artists. Purchasing crafts directly from the people who make them allows buyers to meet the artist and ensure they get the full value of the item. The crafters don't call themselves artists, especially the children, because their effort is too utilitarian—too tied to their survival. Although what they make is crude and would not grace any modern art exhibit, it is nonetheless art in its highest form, conveying meaning that language cannot. We didn't want to pick just one child to buy from and couldn't buy something from all of them, so we apologized as Sisay indifferently shooed the group away.

AFRICA AT 15,000 FEET

"I like the mountains because they make me feel small. They help me sort out what's important in life."
—Mark Obmascik

"Climb that goddamn mountain."
—Jack Kerouac

The windows of the truck had to stay closed, otherwise we would all catch tuberculosis—a common misconception in Ethiopia. The wind is thought by many, especially elders, to spread illness. This has led to many stifling bus rides through the Ethiopian countryside. It is easy to dismiss this belief as ridiculous, but I must remind myself that some people currently think the Earth is flat, and I shouldn't make assumptions on someone's intelligence from a single belief. Anthropologist Jared Diamond calls this "constructive paranoia." Harsh road dust and diesel exhaust from poorly maintained buses have no doubt made many Ethiopians ill. However, these are not issues on a mountain's wet roads and fresh air.

Finally, we were told that we had arrived and could get out of the truck. We didn't need to be told twice. The smell from the rancid goat butter our scout Dawit used as a hair treatment had conspired with the winding road, bringing breakfast to the back of my throat. I gratefully opened the truck door to cool, crisp air. At this elevation in the park, the air always crackled with static, like a thunderstorm was rolling in, even during the dry season. It reminded me of stopping at rest areas on mountain passes back home in Colorado. I felt fortunate to be assigned to a part of Africa with cool weather.

Ras Dejen, the highest point in Ethiopia, was only 10mi (16km) from where we stood, but a massive mile-deep gorge separated us from the roughly 15,000ft (4,600m) high mountain. The gorge's steep sides were draped in torn quilts of rectangular crop fields and terraces. The bright tin roofs of Chiro Leba shone below like scissors cutting through the patchwork of rainfed fields. Any village with *leba* (thief) in its name had a few stories to tell. Unfortunately, we could only watch from a distance. Bwahit Ras, the mountain we stood on and the third highest in Ethiopia, would be as far as we would ever go into the park. Our fruitless efforts with SMNP and government officials inside the park boundary soured future trips farther into the mountains. As Coloradans who enjoyed hiking 14ers—mountains above 14,000ft (4,300m) elevation—we didn't feel the need to summit the highest point in Ethiopia, which was nearly indistinguishable from the surrounding plateau. However, as many other PCVs from Ethiopia and other African countries made the trek, we regretted the decision.

A shadow passed over us. I looked up expecting to see a small, low-flying bird, but instead a bearded vulture with an 8ft (2.5m) wingspan had swooped down silently from a rocky outcropping above. Much in the way that geladas are not really baboons, these beautiful birds are not really vultures. They are as closely related to eagles as they are vultures. Bearded vultures lack the characteristic bald head of other carrion-eaters, and instead of squabbling with scavengers over an animal carcass, they patiently wait for bones to be picked clean for them. Perhaps they would be more appreciated if called "bearded eagle."

Their English name comes from the "beard" of iron-rich mud both male and female birds rub into their naturally white chest feathers. The color is not blood, as some people understandably assume—it is a vulture after all. These birds bathe in red mud. The purpose is still debated, but recent research suggests it is purely cosmetic; making it the only bird in the world that wears rouge. Many other birds are notoriously vain when it comes to sexy dances and decorations to attract mates, but this one puts on makeup.

The puffed out red chests of these large ossivores (bone eaters) are likely worn to dissuade others from taking their territory. Or, they think it just looks cool, which I won't argue. The vulture's Amharic name is translated as "bone-breaker." However, it is better known among Ethiopians and visitors as *lammergeier*. This German misnomer means "lamb-catcher," which the bird doesn't do, and likely comes from the bird's massive size. It also doesn't have the same ring to it as "bone-breaker." Regardless of what you call it, this charismatic bird has an unusual way of eating.

Lammergeier flying. Photo by David Castellano.

We felt lucky to see the lammergeier in action as it flew over the cliff with a bone as long as one of its wings, likely the leg of an ibex. It gracefully tipped a wing as it caught an updraft and glided along a narrow ledge between the clifftop and the valley thousands of feet below. The bone was dropped like a missile toward this ledge as we stared, unblinking. It shattered into two pieces on the rocks, one half cartwheeling off into empty air and the other bouncing to a stop only feet from the edge. Our feathered friend banked casually in a wide circle that led down toward its waiting meal. The lammergeier landed, having never flapped a wing on its long flight from the rocks above. It pulled the cracked bone apart with its strong beak and swallowed the jagged pieces whole. The bird's rugged gullet can handle these meals, along with stomach acid as strong as what is in a car battery. The bird can digest solid bone in less than 24 hours, which is important when your diet is almost exclusively skeletal.

The owner of the Simien Lodge, the only private hotel allowed within the park boundary, mourns the graceful vultures that are electrocuted by the power lines passing through the park. These transmission lines travel along miles of rough terrain to bring power to the isolated village of a government official who advocated for the infrastructure project on "humanitarian grounds." The electricity comes from hydroelectric stations near *Bahir Dar*, capital of the Amhara region, and is transmitted alongside major roads. A dispute involving people from Debark and a neighboring village resulted in the main power line being cut to Debark and the park. There was no power for more than a week.

Massive transmission towers and cables pass directly in front of the Simien Lodge. Every so often, guests are met with the rigid corpses of lammergeier as they stroll from their rooms to enjoy the view on the cliff edge. The broad wings of these avian cleanup crew members allow them to glide in the thin mountain air but are a liability around high-voltage wires. Birds can clip the towers or power lines in blustery winds. An unfortunate few have been electrocuted as their wide wings get too close and cause an electrical arc. The possibility of a grassfire being ignited by the flaming feathers of falling birds is low, but alarmingly not zero.

Fires ignited by lightning were common in the mountains long before humans intentionally set fires or unintentionally turned birds into flying firestarters. Fires have been lit inside the park for centuries to facilitate hunting, flushing out threats (both animal and human), and increasing grass production for livestock. Native species have adapted to occasional fire and can benefit from fires started by humans or natural causes. However, when combined with overgrazing, the fires are harmful because plants and animals aren't allowed time to recover. Fires are also set by beekeepers to smoke hives using burning lichen. While this is done to sedate and confuse the bees, these fires carry a high risk of escaping human control. Escape fires are likely during the dry season—especially on the steep terrain in much of the park. Fires can climb cliffs as flames jump from ledge to ledge.

I witnessed a fire one dry season near Sankaber Camp. Park scouts first noticed the smoke and shot their rifles into the air to alert people to the danger. News of the fire reached a park truck driving from Debark. This truck and a van owned by a local tour guide collected people along the road as they rushed toward the growing black clouds. Local springs and streams had run dry weeks before, and no water was available. Park settlers and scouts used hand tools—shovels, hoes, and picks—to smother the fire with soil. Several people suffered second-degree burns trying to stomp out the fire while barefoot or wearing thin sandals. The fire made it clear that there either wasn't a fire suppression plan in place, people didn't know it, or that it had not been followed.

A fire inside SMNP climbs the steep slopes.

The large human population living in and around the national park creates problems for the park's management because the people living in the area are there illegally, are food insecure, and practice unsustainable farming. This results in the degradation of both the park's ecological health and the ability of poor farmers to grow enough food for themselves. Yet due to the uncertain legal status of park settlers, the park office is limited in its ability to address these problems.

Population remains the most contentious issue in the management of Ethiopia's highland areas, and with good reason.

Almost 90% of Ethiopia's population lives within the country's highlands—areas greater than 5,000ft (1,500m) in elevation. The original park boundary, established in 1969, includes several villages and land that had been cultivated or grazed by local communities for centuries. The UNESCO World Heritage List nomination document states that 80% of the park was under human use. The figure has been more recently reported at 86% of the park being under human use. However, the entirety of the park is affected by human disturbances even if it is not considered to be "in use."

The result has been decades of heated debates over populations that have stifled the effective management of the park up to today. In 1979 and again in 1986, some 1,800 people were forcibly relocated from seven villages on lower slopes. This not only increased tension between local communities and park authorities, it was also ineffective because the villagers returned following the civil unrest in 1991 when relocations were not enforced.

Spurred by the benchmarks required to remove SMNP from the List of World Heritage in Danger, the park boundary was realigned in 2003 and 2004 to exclude perimeter villages. A follow-up study in 2004 estimated that the population growth rate inside the park was 1.5–2.0% per year, which resulted in a doubling of the population every 35 years. While this may seem like a slow increase, each additional birth is another person who depends on the park's already depleted natural resources.

The first major voluntary resettlement of people occurred in 2007, when the village of Arkwasiye was moved 1.2mi (2km) southeast to reestablish it outside the park boundary. Arkwasiye developed as a trading village due to its location in the mountains, and inhabitants primarily relied on trade for their income. The move was voluntary and the impacted villagers were compensated with improved homes, an elementary school, a small health clinic, and a water well. However, a study conducted several years after the move decided that the move resulted in a significant decrease in income and increased stress on local natural resources, because villagers were forced to return to farming for income. The Ethiopian government had gambled that the loss to traditional livelihoods would be offset by tourism jobs. They lost that gamble.

It is important to recognize the negative correlation between education and population growth, especially for girls and women. The average Ethiopian woman with no education wants 4.6 children but ends up having more than 6. Conversely, the average Ethiopian woman with secondary or higher education only wants 1.5 children and has an average of 2. There are other variables in the lives of uneducated women that can lead to higher birth rates; however, the limited educational opportunities inside and adjacent to the park creates a cycle of high births per woman, resulting in poor education for those children due to the costs of raising additional, unplanned children. Except for Chad, Ethiopia has the lowest median age for a woman's first birth in Sub-Saharan Africa. An earlier start to childbearing can have serious health consequences for both mother and child and lengthens a woman's reproductive period, meaning she is more likely to give birth more times in her life. Improving educational opportunities for people living inside the park, especially women, is crucial for reducing the human population pressure on the park's resources.

Despite the undeniable correlation between a large human population and the degradation of land in the Simien Mountains, the uninterrupted decline in the agricultural and ecological value of the park isn't solely caused by increasing human numbers. It is symptomatic of an even larger issue in Ethiopian conservation efforts that little has been done to address—indifference. This statement requires a cultural leap of faith between the values of outcome-oriented Western countries and of the present-oriented, highly traditional Amharan culture.

Concepts of intrinsic natural beauty are modern imports from foreign visitors. The park's first warden, himself a foreigner, recognized this cultural disconnect while speaking to a group of educated Ethiopians on the importance of protecting the park. The Ethiopians thought, "[...] erosion was inevitable. Animals, flowers, and scenery were of little interest. They did not appreciate nature as we did. They did not see it... We were talking into a void." A growing number of educated Ethiopians have a better understanding of ecological principles, but still don't share the Western environmental ethic that caused the park to be listed as a natural World Heritage Site, or even caused the park to be created in the first place.

Degradation can be considered the opposite of sustainability. However, like sustainability, it is subjective and lacks conclusive conditions. The word "degradation" often carries a powerful negative connotation in Western countries. Individuals and organizations who support the park's human residents often refrain from using it when discussing options to manage the park sustainably. This is shortsighted because a key component of sustainability is the continued access to resources. Maintaining a large human presence in the park may keep people close to the resources they have historically used, thereby implying access, but there are fewer resources for each consecutive generation. Supporting the illegal use of the park's declining resources doesn't help the national park or the people living within it.

The traditional Ethiopian system of growing crops relies on expanding cultivated areas to increase overall productivity instead of increasing production on existing fields. Unfortunately, all lands suitable for growing crops, along with many areas not suitable, are already being cultivated. No land is left for farmers to expand onto. Almost 95% of the people in the Simiens are dependent on rain-fed subsistence agriculture. Crop yields from these fields are completely reliant on favorable amounts and timing of rain. Yet rainfall has become more erratic over the past several decades. Meager rainy seasons are more frequent. A rapidly changing climate and poor soil fertility mean that, even in good seasons, on-farm crop production only supplies a maximum of 50% of the local population's annual food requirements. Unreliable growing conditions, declining soil quality, and inadequate productive land for the growing population cause severe food insecurity in the Simien Mountains. These stresses almost guarantee conflict among people, livestock, and wildlife.

    I have heard drought being compared to a fever. Fevers aren't forever and will end eventually—maybe sooner, maybe later, but they will end. However, fevers don't happen in the same deep time that droughts do. Drought is a metastasizing cancer. It grows steadily in the background until the symptoms are bad enough to notice. Symptoms can be treated and prayers for some relief may be answered, but there's no way to know how much worse it will get until it's fatal. Until bones are picked clean and cracked open for the last few scraps.

CLOUDY WITH A CHANCE OF GOATS

"The animals of this world exist for their own reasons. They were not made for humans any more than black people were made for whites."
—Alice Walker

"Animals are, like us, endangered species on an endangered planet, and we are the ones who are endangering them, it, and ourselves. They are innocent sufferers in a hell of our making."
—Jeffrey Moussaieff Masson

Olav Hedberg, a Swedish botanist active in the park in the late 1940s, fittingly wrote the Afroalpine environment was, "Summer every day and winter every night," in reference to the drastic daily temperature swings that vary little with the seasons. The Afroalpine zone, found on the highland plateaus above 12,000ft (3,700m), is dominated by numerous grasses and herbs, but the characteristic giant lobelias are the most visible. Their straight, bare trunks and high tuft of fleshy leaves make them look like Truffula trees dreamt up by a prehistoric Dr. Seuss. While many of their neighbors evolved to hug the ground to adapt to the harsh, high-elevation environment, giant lobelias take the opposite approach. By having a tall growth habit, the lobelia can escape drastic daily temperature changes that happen close to the ground. How tall? They often top out at 20ft (6m), but some reach up to 30ft (9m) high when they flower.

Derek standing 6ft (1.8m) tall next to a giant lobelia plant.

Unfortunately, over 95% of their habitat is under threat by extreme weather changes and land clearing for agriculture.

The fragile alpine areas of the national park provide habitat for many of Ethiopia's most well-known and threatened wildlife, such as the Walia ibex and Ethiopian wolf. The large, flat expanses of alpine grass are also heavily used by domestic livestock. These fragile Afroalpine pastures provide almost half of the total livestock feed grown in the park. Overgrazing from livestock has degraded these incomparable ecosystems into isolated tufts of grass surrounded by bare rocks and gullies.

The protection of the charismatic Walia ibex is one of the original reasons for the creation of the SMNP and has been a symbol of Ethiopian wildlife conservation for decades. The ibex's face is the logo of the Ethiopian Wildlife Conservation Authority (EWCA), and its conservation is a "do-or-die" objective for the agency. A local legend attributes the arrival of Walia ibex into the Simien Mountains to the Orthodox Christian Saint Yared, who used the animal to carry his holy books around Ethiopia. Although doubtful, the story does reveal a deep cultural appreciation that has helped save the goat from extinction.

In 1972, only 105 ibex remained in the area, according to the Frankfurt Zoological Society. The population is slowly increasing, but these impressive goats are still listed as a vulnerable species by the International Union for Conservation of Nature (IUCN). As of 2020, less than 600 mature ibex were present in the wild. Most of the population inhabits areas in the park with relatively little disturbance from humans, such as around Chennek Camp. Some park staff credit the population increase to harsh fines and strict enforcement against hunting ibex. The ibex population plummeted during the Ethiopian Civil War when poaching and disturbance from rebel groups was high and there was no way to enforce hunting rules. The species was listed as critically endangered and at high risk of extinction after the war. Thankfully, it is now highly unlikely that the Walia ibex will become extinct if present conservation measures are continued and assuming climatic changes will not drastically affect existing habitat.

Humans are not the only hunters ibex need to worry about. Enough goats must reach adulthood to compensate for losses from natural predators. Adult ibex can be caught by hyenas at lower elevations, but ibex kids are the most vulnerable. Hyenas, leopards, and Ethiopian wolves can easily catch young ibex that don't make it in time to a cliff. Predators cannot follow, and the goats use their strong hooves to stick to the near-vertical walls. Surprisingly, one of the greatest risks to these nimble climbers is the spread of disease from domestic sheep and goats that graze the same areas.

We were living in Debark when two leopards were stoned to death in less than six months near the Limalimo scout camp. Both pelts were brought to the park office to demonstrate that the animals were not poached for their valuable hide. Although there was some element of regret when the second leopard was killed, both park staff and warden supported killing the leopard because it was accused of killing two sheep. The first leopard, however, was killed simply because it was considered too close to a village. When I asked a park scout why it had been killed, he quickly replied, "It eats people."

When people in the rural areas outside Debark are asked if leopards attack humans, they emphatically say yes. If pressed about details of actual events, the responses instantly become ambiguous, citing events in other areas or from many years in the past. The elusive cats are not endangered, but their population is declining. It is nearly impossible to create accurate surveys of leopards because they are so well camouflaged, are mainly nocturnal, and avoid human settlements. Most elderly

Walia ibex walking at high elevation in the Simien Mountains.

park residents I interviewed admitted to never having seen one. The network of game cameras set by the gelada researchers at Sankaber captured a single, rare image of a leopard only once during our time in Ethiopia. Regardless, the concept of leopards attacking humans seemed to be ingrained in the local culture, and an animosity toward the elusive animals had been cultivated over generations. It will be difficult to ever find a balance between the threatened cats and the rural people.

When it comes to conservation efforts, the second most famous mammal in the park is not as secure as the Walia ibex, and so its killings of ibex young are tolerated. The Ethiopian wolf, also known as the Simien wolf, Ethiopian red fox, or any combination thereof, is endangered, and its numbers are dropping. The Amharic name for the wolf is *kay kabaro*, translated as "red fox," which is well-suited to its orange coat and slender snout. The park office estimated the local wolf population at only 102 in 2012, but this had dropped to an estimated 75 in 2023. This is up from the 20 to 30 wolves surveyed by the Frankfurt Zoological

Society in 1997, but still represents a highly vulnerable population.

The Ethiopian wolf is the rarest canid (dog) on Earth, and its population is estimated to be below 500. All live within Ethiopia, dispersed among seven small, isolated populations which weakens the gene pool. DNA analysis suggests that the Ethiopian wolf is more closely related to the gray wolf and the coyote than to any African canid; likely having evolved from a gray wolf-like ancestor that arrived from Eurasia. It represents an extremely unique branch of the canine family tree and a highlight of any trip in the Simien Mountains.

The main prey of the Ethiopian wolf are rodents, such as mole rats, that have adapted to the extreme weather of the Ethiopian highlands. The small range of important prey species for the wolf limits the range of the wolf itself. Rabies and distemper outbreaks spread by domestic dogs have decimated Ethiopian wolf populations in both the Bale Mountains—on the other side of the Rift Valley—and the Simien Mountains in recent decades. Such outbreaks have killed up to three quarters of isolated wolf populations in Ethiopia. Outbreaks in the Simien Mountains can result in regional extinction because the local population lacks the numbers to recover. It is difficult for wolves to recover from disease outbreaks because livestock eat what the wolves' prey eat. Overgrazing has been killing the wolves for decades as the number of prey animals declines. Despite its highly endangered status and vulnerability to disease outbreaks, there are no captive breeding programs anywhere in the world because the Ethiopian government has refused to authorize such a program.

Conflicts between wildlife and humans are a common problem in Ethiopia. Both imperialist Ethiopia and the Derg regime were coercive when it came to managing the country's natural resources. All private land was seized and nationalized. Existing government property, such as state forests, were expanded to gobble up neighboring land—forcing out entire communities. These actions quickly turned communities against the idea of conserving the environment for the public good. By reducing or eliminating benefits from communal lands, the government soured many rural Ethiopians on the potential benefits to managing natural areas sustainably. It is challenging for both the government and rural communities to go from a system of violent compliance to a system of participation and shared benefits.

Throughout Ethiopia's protected areas—not just the Simien Mountains—most residents believe that wildlife and humans can coexist. However, villagers who have not directly benefited from protected areas are much less likely to respond positively toward wildlife. More local benefits from protected areas means more local support. Residents who don't think humans and wildlife can coexist are more likely to have experienced financial loss from wildlife. Owners of large livestock herds are less likely to support protecting wildlife because they are more likely to experience predation from wildlife. Similarly, families without income from additional sources, such as tourism or hired labor, are less likely to support wildlife protection because every loss from predation or competition for grazing land is a threat to their survival.

One of the ways SMNP is offering benefits to local communities is through the government's use of park revenue for improving educational opportunities in and around the park. Most of Ethiopia's protected areas are in rural parts of the country.

Residents who live in or near these areas are often illiterate and have few educational opportunities compared to people in cities. One of the best ways to support local environmental conservation is to improve educational opportunities for local Ethiopians, because there is a strong positive relationship between a person's education and their support for conservation goals. Ethiopians with access to higher quality education are more likely to understand the long-term economic and ecological importance of Ethiopia's natural areas.

In addition to receiving a small portion of government revenue from tourism, schools in Debark have benefited from tourist-led philanthropic projects. When appropriately planned with local families, these projects can provide lasting benefits beyond making volunteers feel good about themselves. Millennium High School is the larger of the two secondary schools around the park. It was built in commemoration of the Ethiopian millennium in 2007 through collaboration between a local community foundation and several Dutch philanthropists.

Along with providing these funds, a group of Dutch tourists spent 12 days working with local community members to build two new classroom blocks. Without the labor and financial support from tourists, the school may not have ever been built. Although a market town, Debark is considered urban by Ethiopian standards. Rural areas are much less likely to share in the benefits because they are less accessible and harder to protect from opportunistic looters. Villages in the park are at an even greater disadvantage because people are technically living there illegally. The Simien Lodge and Limalimo Lodge both provide employment opportunities in rural areas and give back to the community by directing tourism dollars outside Debark.

It can be challenging to be optimistic about the future of people and wildlife in the Simien Mountains. For those paying attention to the trends, it can feel like time is running out to protect the park for future generations. For better and worse, the grinding decline of the park's ability to support life is a problem of shifting baselines. Most changes are not visible year-to-year. A visitor may think the park looks gorgeous (and rightfully so) and that everything is as it should be. They would be alarmed, however, if they could see the park's condition 5, 10, or 20 years before.

All the "targets," "goals," and "desired outcomes" don't mean anything unless plans to reach these objectives are developed alongside them. The problems in instituting the park's General Management Plan are similar to the difficulties in fulfilling the UN Millennium Development Goals (MDG), international goals for improving the lives of the world's poorest people. Both are undeniably steps toward a more sustainable future for the people that the documents are meant to benefit. Although, the park's plan has a much narrower scope (i.e. not the entirety of mankind). The MDGs have been criticized for being a grocery list of ingredients for cooking up a better world, but unfortunately not many people want to take the time or money to buy those ingredients. In the end, so many substitutions and omissions have been made by governments and organizations that the resulting metaphoric culinary disaster will be, in the best case, edible, but certainly not palatable.

The SMNP's plan is a grocery list for a more ecologically and economically resilient park, but like the UN goals, no one is willing to invest in what is needed to see the document fully enacted. The 2012 MDG Report is littered with comments like, "Target is still out of reach," "Gains were very limited," and "Progress has slowed." Failure to meet the original eight goals was met by swift action in 2015…by renaming them the Sustainable Development Goals (SDG) and increasing their number to 17. The park faces a just as drastic failure to meet its stated goals. Those who have not experienced the management structure of the park might embrace the plan as a straightforward roadmap to success. Those who do have such experience, however, can do little more than sigh and say, "I'll do what I can."

SOMETHING WICKED THIS WAY COMES

"Loyalty to petrified opinions never yet broke a chain or freed a human soul in this world—and never will."

—Mark Twain

"If democracy is to mean anything at all, then experts and laypeople have to solve complicated problems together. First, however, they have to overcome the widening gulf between them."

—Thomas M. Nichols

I stepped out onto our narrow stoop, letting the coffee grounds settle in my mug before taking a sip. Eucalyptus leaves burning in open cookfires created an aromatic smoke that hugged the ground. The cloying haze was obtrusive but not unpleasant. Women were cooking in the compound behind us. I didn't know the occasion, but it was probably some saint's feast day—a seemingly daily occurrence. Unrestrained laughter floated over our thin wall of split wood and rusty nails. The laughter carried with it the gamey smell of goat meat simmering in a spicy stew. These odors mingled with coffee percolating in clay jebena pots, fresh horse droppings, human urine, laundry detergent flakes, and dry-season road dust.

A crackling call to prayer was played over the speaker system of a nearby mosque. The top of its minaret was just visible over the tin roofs of the surrounding houses. The singsong call to prayer was met with the braying of an overworked donkey and the crowing of a loose rooster that escaped the fate of the goat next door. I could hear a group of children pass by, kicking a well-worn soccer ball between them. This cacophony of sounds and smells was gentle but jarring. The ebb and flow of village life never ended. It was like the traditional beehives nestled in a tree at the end of our street, always buzzing, never still—alive. Life in rural Africa was chaotic, but with recognizable patterns that repeated over and over and over again. The community was awash in these familiar sights, sounds, and smells that tied everything and everyone together.

Community is more than just an abstract group of people. Community is a verb. It is dynamic, intricate, and difficult to define. As in so many other communities, the complex, interrelated

Transferring bees from a traditional hive to a modern hive during a Peace Corps training.

challenges that threaten the Simien Mountains cannot be resolved only by changing policy at a national level. These challenges must be addressed by local communities to be improved. The goal is a strong legal and social framework for managing resources. But that goal can only be met by empowering local land managers to make decisions that are culturally appropriate AND scientifically accurate.

This is called participatory management. Instead of relying on top-down decision making, participatory management empowers community members to be active in planning and decisions that impact them. Instead of a distant head office dictating activities, local stakeholders create and conduct local projects. Stakeholders can be local park staff, but also private guides or people living in the park. This management philosophy works by valuing local knowledge, highlighting local assets and needs, and developing local capacity to address those needs. Community participation can raise community confidence and build a better framework for managing challenges equitably and effectively.

Participation can be interpreted in several different ways, but those involved should agree that participation must be voluntary to be beneficial. Forced participation is not participation, it is obligation. Playing the Monopoly board game can be fun (arguably), but forcing someone to play often ends in tears, scattered game pieces, and no one winning. On the other hand, extending opportunities for voluntary participation has been shown to increase equity within communities. A Ford Foundation study demonstrated that participation can help resolve problems between groups with uneven power. For example, a cutthroat child who owns the Monopoly Boardwalk space and is demanding rent from their sibling who has already mortgaged all of their properties...or something like that. Maybe I'm just still mad at my brother.

In the real world, this is done by increasing transparency and confronting power inequalities without judgment. This is especially valuable when trying to make decisions about potentially conflicting land uses, such as pristine wildlife habitat, livestock pasture, or a tourism hotspot. The power inequality between rural agriculturalists, the tourists traveling to experience those resources, and the government offices charged with managing those resources is on full display in Ethiopia—with fingers pointing in all directions.

Yet, participatory management is notoriously challenging to develop and sustain. Some participants may not see the power differences as an issue and won't want to challenge the status quo. Environmental decisions in the Simien Mountains are often decided communally, with groups of elders approving or disapproving of individuals' decisions. Conservation involves the distribution of benefits from scarce resources, as a result, these resources are often owned or utilized by people with financial or political power. In the Simien Mountains, these are usually elders with political connections or people favored by these elders. This power dynamic is common worldwide and is why many environmental projects in developing countries include objectives to evenly distribute program benefits. However, these interventions can further marginalize individuals or groups if facilitators don't identify and engage people that lack political or economic leverage.

Local empowerment is a requirement, not a feel-good goal, for rural communities to successfully manage the environments they rely on to survive. By building on existing community resources and equipping local people with new techniques or insights, participatory management can help create local partners who are confident and knowledgeable. For development projects to be self-supporting beyond initial funding and facilitation, the local community must be involved in planning, implementing, and evaluating them. Many project funders and facilitators have taken this for granted or largely downplayed the importance of local input.

The Food for Work (FFW) conservation programs in the Simien Mountains are a perfect example of poor local participation in projects and how that limits project success. Miles of stone-walled terraces intended to conserve soil have been built throughout the mountains. However, these stone structures can house large populations of rats which devour much of a farmer's crop. To compensate for this loss, many farmers are forced to buy rat poison, which is expensive and often ends up poisoning Ethiopian wolves which are natural predators of the rats.

One farmer near Mekane Berhan, southeast of Debark, didn't want walls on his land because he knew the potential problems posed by the structures. Nevertheless, a large group of people from a government-led Food for Work project came and built them anyway. The resulting stone structures not only harbored a large rat population, but also made it difficult for the farmer to work his fields. Despite the large investment in these "conservation" structures, many were dismantled by farmers or left to collapse back into the fields. If local farmers had been allowed to participate in planning conservation projects, such costly and inefficient mistakes may have been avoided.

The most pressing problems facing the Simien Mountains have eluded their proposed solutions for decades. Problems often end up worsening instead of being solved, such as the FFW stone walls project and the forced resettlement of people from within the park that took place in the 1980s. That is because these issues are "wicked problems."

Planning and design theorists Rittel and Webber (1973) identified ten common characteristics of wicked problems:

1. There is no definitive formulation of the problem; differing values influence the defining of the problem.
2. There is no stopping rule; there are no criteria that let the decision-makers know that a solution has been found.
3. Solutions to wicked problems are not true-or-false, but good-or-bad.
4. There is no immediate and no ultimate test of a solution to a wicked problem; there is no clear way to test the outcome of a solution before it is implemented.
5. Every solution to a wicked problem is a one-shot operation; every attempt to solve the problem changes the problem itself and eliminates the possibility of trial-and-error solutions.
6. There is not a finite set of potential solutions to operate from; the best possible solution may not even be identified before a solution must be implemented.
7. Every wicked problem is essentially unique; the unique components of the problems make it difficult to generalize about other problems.
8. Every wicked problem can be considered to be a symptom of another problem; wicked problems are often an expression of a group of problems and therefore multiple systematic and holistic solutions are necessary.

9. The explanation for the problem's existence influences the problem's resolution; there may be multiple explanations of a problem and therefore multiple resolutions.
10. Problem-solvers are not allowed to be wrong; they are pressured to make decisions that have little to no chance of leading to a desirable outcome.

You have likely encountered wicked problems in your own life. They are not unique to developing countries. Well-intentioned, and apparently well-planned, attempts to resolve wicked problems often result in polarized and entrenched positions on important issues. Instead of people forming solutions on middle ground, people take sides and retreat to their corners where they dig in their feet, unwilling to compromise or consider others' ideas. Purely rational attempts to solve the SMNP's problems have fallen short due to the opposing values that define project targets. Italian sociologist Luigi Pellizzoni points out that when there appears to be enough evidence to support one position over another, stakeholders emphasize different facts, or give them different interpretations. There isn't agreement on the relevant information or even the principles at stake. Facts and values overlap. Different factions within the park population and government staff are constantly trying to pull the park's management in different directions.

The park's first warden hinted at the wicked nature of the park's problems before the concept of wicked problems was written, when he said,

> "The problems of malnutrition, the lack of education and understanding, the poor farming and erosion, the disease and corruption were all in turn problems of the

national park. They were all interrelated, just like the complicated blood-relationships of the local people."

To achieve participation with the Simien people that still accomplishes conservation goals, it is necessary to teach them not just how their environment can be conserved, but why it should be. Too often, farmers inside the park see soil erosion as an inevitable, unstoppable natural occurrence, falling crop yields as an act of God or black magic, and trampled grasslands the result of weak grass instead of overgrazing. Wicked problems are part of the society they arise from. Any attempt at resolution brings with it a call for changes in that society. That change starts with two-way education. People must be able to recognize when problems can be changed through their choices. Participation is needed to engage community members and promote those changes.

Despite all the potential benefits of highly participatory projects, there are sizable potential drawbacks as well. The most blatant issue of participation for the national park is that all residents are there illegally. It is against Ethiopian law to live in or even use the resources of Ethiopia's protected areas without direct approval. To include park residents in decision-making would be granting them some legitimacy, which the government does not want to happen.

A common dilemma with participatory projects in Ethiopia is the pay-for-participation mentality. International Non-Governmental Organizations (NGOs) have a long history of providing per diem pay for local Ethiopian participants to increase stakeholder involvement, particularly involvement from poor stakeholders. This has created a bizarre focus-group type of participation where locals are paid to sit in a room and talk about a particular subject. The basis for this pay-for-participation system appears sound. Participation in trainings or meetings can force people to forgo other opportunities for income or enjoyment. Paying them provides an immediate incentive for stakeholders that might otherwise not be able to afford to take the time away from these other activities.

This method creates problems when the amount participants are paid and the scheduling of participatory programs don't take local pay rates and seasonal schedules into account. For attending one afternoon of meetings, participants are commonly paid upward of five days' worth of wages for day laborers, and well over a week's worth of work for rural farmers. This overvaluation of attendance literally pays for participants' thoughts in a forced environment that can be skewed by the goals of foreign facilitators and the desire to tell them what participants think they want to hear.

In addition to the Community Needs Assessment done at the beginning of my Peace Corps service, I led several other participatory appraisal activities during my 27 months in Ethiopia. Participatory appraisal is a community-based approach to actionable research that recognizes people as experts in their own lives and allows them to prioritize the issues important to them. This sounds intuitive, but many development organizations force foreign priorities and solutions onto local problems, while at the same time "mining" local experience to rationalize their approach.

Highly inclusive decision-making may lead to lengthy deliberations, decreased trust among stakeholders and facilitators, and increased controversy and conflict. All these problems have been witnessed at community meetings in the park office. Making participatory decision-making a priority for issues inside the park, delays the implementation of potential solutions for weeks, months, or forever. This strains budgets,

Derek conducting a project development training for SMNP staff.

schedules, stakeholder interest, and the patience of all involved. The price of participation may be high but is often necessary for wicked problems to be resolved. Some of the projects that are put off indefinitely are ones that never should have been proposed, or at least never made mandatory, such as the rat-condo stone walls of the FFW project.

The terms "community" and "participation" have existed in international development circles for several decades. However, the concepts have reached critical mass. The UN development goals, and numerous other targets of human well-being, include opportunities for participation as an indicator of human welfare. Participation and community have become abundant buzzwords in conference proceedings, mission statements, goals, objectives, and organizational visions of government agencies and nonprofit NGOs.

Despite the overuse of such concepts as "participatory" and "community," it is important to realize that they have become overused for a reason. They are necessary for effectively managing the land, water, and life that people rely on for their survival. The costs of participation are not optional, especially if they are treated that way.

EROSION

"I don't need to read between the lines of endless reports to see the country's severe population, health and environment challenges—they are visible in the protruding ribcages of the cattle and the barren eroding terraces in the nation's rural highlands."
—Geoffrey D. Dabelko

"A hungry stomach has no ears."
—Jean de La Fontaine

The population of Ethiopia will fly past 130 million by 2025 at current growth rates, doubling about every 28 years. We can debate the merits and disadvantages of international aid for decades (and we have), but the sad fact—yes, I will call it a fact—is that Ethiopia cannot survive as a functional society without transfusions of funding from foreign sources. If aid stops, people die. If aid continues, people die. They will die more slowly and in greater numbers. The mission to end poverty in Ethiopia, and all of Africa, will not be fulfilled in this generation or the next. What is now a global problem is gradually becoming an African problem.

A 2019 report from the World Bank applauds the reduction in the share of Africans living in extreme poverty from 54% in 1990 to 41% in 2015. If trends continue, the African poverty rate should drop to a miraculous 23% by 2030. Unfortunately, the continent's population growth rate is higher, and the number of people living in poverty has increased from 278 million in 1990 to 413 million in 2015. A lower percentage of a much larger number is not a victory for those left behind. A rising tide raises the ships already above water—the rest are anchored to the seafloor. Based on these trends, Africa will be home to 90% of the world's poor by 2030. Despite rapid economic growth, abject poverty will make its last stand in Africa.

Fifty years ago, the first warden of the park lamented,

> "Disaster was surely inevitable for the Simien people. They had raped the land, the soil was impoverished and eroded away. Streams and rivers were dying, and springs killed [...] Already the people were barely surviving on what they raised. By destroying what remained, they could not last more than fifty years."

This prediction was pessimistic, but agricultural conditions have gotten worse since C.W. Nicol penned those words. While local agricultural production continuously falls short of demand, food aid has allowed the Simien people to stay in the mountains.

Historically, the once prosperous kingdom of Axum declined in the 700s from loss of trade to the Persians. However, the nail in the kingdom's coffin was exploitation of the soil. Intensive tillage and deforestation led to erosion and the conversion of once productive cropland into desert. The dry, gullied landscape of the Ethiopian highlands is not natural.

Unsustainable agricultural practices in the Simiens continue today, especially in upland areas such as Gich. The ratio of soil erosion to new soil formation is 10 to 15 times higher than what is sustainable on the average cultivated slope. Soil productivity is declining 3% annually due to the land degradation in the area. Insecure land tenure discourages land users from investing time and money on the land they cultivate or graze—why invest if you might lose it the next season?

Using dung as an energy source and construction material

A Debark woman travels through eucalyptus trees and over eroded ravines to fill her water jug.

instead of using it as a fertilizer, causes significant agricultural and ecological problems. For every 220lbs (100kg) of dung used for fuel instead of fertilizer, a reduced crop yield of 40–45lbs (18–20kg) can be expected. This adds up to a very sizable reduction. In the Simien region, this crop loss can be as high as 400–880lbs (181–400kg) per household per year, higher than losses from wildlife. While the floor and interior walls of nearly every private building in Debark are covered in manure plaster, the material does add both strength and flexibility. The smell was never bad, even sometimes pleasant, except for when it was freshly applied.

Low investments in soil health, unpredictable crop yields, and a history of food aid distributions have led to dependency on international food aid. Research from the Frankfurt Zoological Society reveals many people living in or around SMNP are dependent on food aid for up to six months out of the year. If not done carefully, food aid disincentivizes local food production by lowering its price below the cost to grow it. Thoughtfully withdrawing food aid in Ethiopia could ultimately improve aid recipients' welfare by spurring domestic food production instead of suppressing it.

When food aid is expected, but arrives late, it reduces the ability of its recipients to develop ways to cope during local food shortages. It is counterintuitive, but food aid can make famine more likely. Instead of finding local alternatives or even migrating, people in the region continue to rely on external aid—even when its delivery is reactionary and comes too late to be beneficial. Additionally, aid has been shown to hasten population growth and simultaneously reduce investments in human capital in Sub-Saharan Africa. A well-intentioned, yet poorly conceived work-for-food program in Dabat Town, located just south of Debark, directly contributed to increased birth rates among beneficiary households. Larger aid allowances for larger families motivated families to have more children so they could receive more aid, which was greater than the perceived cost of having additional children.

An Ethiopian aid worker tried to explain it to me this way. Time as a resource and childhood as a period of inherent value are two of the most important abstract ideas in Western cultures. Time is money, and childhood is more than pre-adult training. This is not the case in Ethiopia. Time and children just happen. Time is not something that can be saved or spent, just as the financial cost of raising a child is not something that can be accounted for. This difference is surprisingly difficult to articulate, and any resulting confusion is the friction from foreign mindsets rubbing as they pass. Getting paid for each child in the house is direct and immediate, but the money required to raise that child is indirect and simply a cost of life.

It would be shortsighted to declare food aid detrimental to people receiving it. Food aid has been shown to provide considerable benefits to recipients when it is targeted and properly timed. But doing it right is tough. A World Bank study concluded that 85% of all Western aid in the 20th century was not used for what it was intended. Unless there is an active, life-threatening emergency, aid should be intended to fill gaps and supplement food systems, not replace them.

For example, flooding a local market with free grain during an emergency not only provides food where there is none, it also creates a ripple effect of depressed local prices, which benefits poorer people by making food more affordable. However, it doesn't benefit the farmers who grow, transport, or sell the food. The complex food systems people have built to survive will collapse if this goes on for too long. Goosing the food supply in this way can save lives in the short term but can undermine the ability of recipient countries to save their own lives in the long term. Food aid is the nuclear option of international altruism.

While humanitarian reasons are the basis for food aid, especially in Africa, there is a growing body of evidence that suggests food aid is also largely motivated by political and economic gains for the donors. In 2007, researchers revealed that food aid deliveries to Ethiopia were driven by wheat prices in the USA and had very little to do with the level of grain production in Ethiopia. More recent evidence has shown that food aid policies are often driven by benefits to farmers in donor countries instead of aid recipients in food-insecure countries. This combination of altruistic and self-serving reasons for providing food aid means that food aid will likely be an issue in the Simien Mountains for the foreseeable future.

International tourist attractions in developing countries, such as the Simien Mountains, often have high local need and high visibility for foreigners. This potent combination lowers the likelihood of food aid distribution being slowed in the park any time soon because potential food aid supporters are put in direct contact with potential food aid recipients. Foreign visitors' support for food aid distribution may unintentionally cause further degradation of the plants and wildlife that made them select the Simien Mountains for their travel. The most apparent example of this is the road that was laid directly through the park, which was originally built to facilitate food aid distribution to more remote communities. In an unfortunate case of poor collaboration, UNESCO and the UN Emergency Unit for Ethiopia (UN-EUE) were found on opposite ends of the aid issue. While UNESCO has vehemently and consistently called for the relocation of settlements inside and adjacent to the park, the UN-EUE was a strong supporter of constructing the road through the park to facilitate food aid to the same people.

The road accelerated settlement inside the park by making it easier to supply once isolated settlements. I spoke to several people who moved inside the park, motivated by expected compensation from the Ethiopian government or a foreign donor if a resettlement program was ever carried out within the park boundary. The road through the park was an uncontrolled means of transportation for people and materials through the park, and multiple ecological problems with the road were identified in the park's general management plan as early as 2008. After the road was completed, the UN-EUE abruptly recognized the damage from this "food aid highway." The organization now acknowledges that the road not only causes direct ecological damage through erosion and wildlife habitat fragmentation, but that it also "destroys the resources of ecotourism, which is one of the few, if not the only dollar-earning industry in this part of Ethiopia."

Since the predecessor of the US Agency for International Development (USAID) began giving aid to Ethiopia in 1952, billions of dollars have been provided, with almost 2 billion dollars in 2022 and 2023 alone. Ethiopia has remained one of the primary recipients of non-military aid from the USA for decades. Other developed countries also open their coffers for millions of dollars in development assistance and humanitarian aid.

The salaries and office equipment of many agricultural office employees are directly funded by USAID or other US-backed development institutions. I heard stories of the dedication of some of these workers and read about the work they did toward creating an ecologically and economically strong future for Ethiopia. I never personally saw such workers in action. More than once, I visited an agricultural office to find only one computer, of many, with a power cable attached. This was used to play either Minesweeper or Solitaire. The other computers sat untouched under yellowing plastic dust covers—reduced to totems of functional governance.

Over 80% of the humanitarian funding to Ethiopia between 2005 and 2009 was for emergency food aid, while barely half a percent of the funding for the same period was for disaster preparedness. This figure may be dated, but the trends continue. Only a fraction of humanitarian funding flowing into Ethiopia, including the Simien region, went toward reducing the country's vulnerability to events that necessitated emergency food aid in the first place. Governments that know food aid shipments can be relied upon in times of famine will limit investments in sustainable agricultural methods, further decreasing the country's food security.

The human population within the SMNP boundary and the park buffer zone has weakened traditional livelihoods and threatened the region's ecotourism potential. Even though the value of wildlife conservation, scenic beauty, natural heritage, and tourism far exceeds the value of the park as an agricultural production area, farming and grazing are given priority over all other management concerns. Aid agencies must very carefully evaluate the effects of food aid in the Simien Mountains and determine the best long-term solutions for the residents of the region, even if that means the cessation of food aid.

Although the grazing of livestock is directly tied to peoples' livelihoods in the park, livestock pose a particularly insidious problem for the park office because grazing negatively affects both the environmental and economic value of the park. In addition to being one of the largest contributors to soil erosion, among a host of other ecological problems, the Ethiopian livestock sector is lacking in both quality and quantity. Ethiopian economist Dr. Ayele Kuris points out that despite having the largest livestock population in Africa, the third largest livestock population in the world, and with more than half of Ethiopia's land mass used for grazing, the country's livestock sector's performance is poor even by African standards.

Grazing in the Simien Mountains is part of a diverse subsistence strategy and has cultural implications for the people living in the park, even if it is illegal. However, as stated in the park's General Management Plan,

> "SMNP cannot ignore the needs of the impoverished communities living in and within its boundaries, but the long-term future of both the SMNP and these communities is in jeopardy in the current situation."

Grazing pressure is estimated to be three times more than land in the park can support. The current level of livestock grazing in and around the park brings added challenges for its management because raising livestock is a volatile livelihood strategy that places people inside the park at risk, it brings numerous environmental problems, and it decreases the value of the park for tourism.

However, research on the economic value of Ethiopian livestock has revealed two ways livestock are important beyond the direct sale of animals or animal products. First, livestock can be used as an alternative to borrowing money from banks or individuals. The interest on loans to smallholders is often exorbitant, and selling part of a herd is usually a better choice when large amounts of money are needed. Second, livestock are a form of insurance for unexpected expenses.

Regardless, the importance of livestock for the people living inside or nearby the park is moot. High numbers and poor management of these animals have created a downward spiral that becomes less productive every year. According to livestock owners in the park, increasing domestic animals in the park has not improved livelihoods. Irreversible damage is already occurring throughout the park. The Ethiopian government must choose to either maintain the park for mediocre farming or as an actual national park. At one point, a path existed for both, but poor management made them mutually exclusive. Ecologists have an obligation to limit the risks associated with potentially grave threats to welfare. Livestock are part of the culture in the Simien Mountains, and ecologists who support alternative ways for people to make a living are not challenging traditional agriculture at their expense. Such ecologists are fulfilling an obligation to reduce the risks that threaten not only individual species, but also all the resources vulnerable people rely upon for their survival.

The most precious of these resources is water. This is true for both humans and animals, wild and domestic. The Simien Mountains catch and direct water that affects a large part of East Africa. The mountains are an important catchment for the Tekeze

River which is used downstream by millions of people in Ethiopia and Sudan. The Tekeze and the Blue Nile are the only perennial rivers in the region—with all other rivers flowing only 3–6 months a year. Restoring and protecting these rivers is crucial for people, plants, and animals. No one likes begging for water.

Tree heather falling into deep gully erosion inside SMNP.

PART III

RUNNING DRY

"When the well is dry, we will know the worth of water."
—Benjamin Franklin

*"Water links us to our neighbor in a
way more profound and complex than any other."*
—John Thorson

"*Ezi-bet...Ezi-bet...EZI-BET!?*" Selam shouted at the closed door, "Is anyone here!?"

No one answered. The residents must not have been home because we would have been able to see them moving around through the large gaps in the sweat-polished eucalyptus poles that made up the front door. We continued to the next house.

Once again, our neighbor Selam called out to see if anyone was there to help us. *One-Mississippi...what if the water is shut off here too? Two-Mississippi...is this normally what she does when she runs out of water, or is she just doing it for Claire and me? Three-Mississippi...did we bring enough money to fill our jugs? Four-Mississippi...how many more people are going to stop to watch what we are doing? Five-Mississippi...how many times are we going to have to do this?*

Finally, a small, hunched man on the other side of the door sighed and unhurriedly opened it. He looked at Selam with a blank expression, then turned to face me with a look of pure incomprehension, as if hallucinating. His unblinking eyes didn't turn back to Selam until she greeted him a second time. She explained that, like many in our cluster of compounds, the water line in our area was off for over two weeks, our storage system of buckets and barrels had run dry days ago. We heard the water had been turned on in this part of town just an hour before. *May we please use your water tap to fill up our jugs? We will pay double what he paid.*

The old man, who introduced himself as Abay, gave us a crooked smile and said we would be welcome to fill our jugs if the water was still on. Abay asked us to wait while he went to check.

Selam looked at me and snorted a quick laugh. "He did not think ferenj when he open door," she said in English.

Abay wasn't expecting a white guy wearing Ethiopian clothes to knock on his door, understandably. He returned to say the water was still on but that we should hurry…it could be shut off any minute. Ten gallons was hardly worth taking payment for, but Abay stared at each coin that Selam pinched into his hand. It would at least be enough for a cup of tea or t'ella.

Abay led us through his two-room house and into the back of the compound where the tap was. He checked again to make sure the tap was working and went inside while the jugs were filling. He returned seconds later to invite us for his wife to prepare coffee for us. I was about to reluctantly accept the offer when Selam said we needed to return with the water so that her Aunt Dinkenesh could begin cooking dinner—a reasonable excuse to decline. She was as tired as I was from chasing the water around town, and we still needed to walk back.

This was normally the work of an Ethiopian girl, filling the repurposed five-gallon oil jug with water and carrying it all the way home, potentially over several miles. A full jug weighs around 45lbs (20kg), too awkward and heavy to carry using the single, small handle built into its top. Years of practice and strength-building allow young women to balance these jugs on their head, with only a folded cloth for cushioning. It is impossible not to be impressed when they lift and carry a sloshing jug—weighing half as much as they do—and casually walk barefoot over rocky dirt roads. I would have been more in awe of the strength it took if they didn't do it with so much grace.

I tried gripping the handle with both hands, but it was too short. Carrying the jug that way would have required me to awkwardly hold it out in front or straddle it while I walked. This was during the dry season while I recovered from my dysentery. My gut was fine, but I still had pounds of muscle to rebuild. The first failed attempts to carry the jug were admittedly hilarious. By the time we had gotten only ten yards from the water tap, a small group of children had gathered to watch the spectacle of a white guy losing a fight with a bright-yellow plastic jug. My face was red in equal parts embarrassment and effort. *This isn't going to work*. Annoyed and unsure what to do, I decided to ham it up. I made a show of the jug being stuck to the ground, completely immovable no matter what I tried. The children squealed with laughter as I stepped back and dramatically wiped my brow, dripping sweat by now—my involuntary commitment to theatrical realism. Some boys ran back and forth miming my failed attempts to carry the water between my legs, looking like they were riding invisible, uncooperative donkeys.

Selam laughed too, but it wasn't all comedy. She lowered her head toward me and nodded slightly, half in affirmation and half in defeat. She called one of the older girls over and instructed her to carry my water. The girl, no more than 12, hustled over with a smile, let Selam set the jug on her head, and accompanied us home with a friend. Selam carried her own water jug the whole way, and the two younger girls traded off carrying my water jug. They didn't trade off because it was too heavy, but rather because they both wanted to help.

We stopped at the fence of eucalyptus poles that separated my compound from that of Selam's family. Selam lowered her water to the ground and helped bring my jug down. I told the girls to wait and ducked into my compound. Claire was reading on our goat-hide bench and stared at me perplexed as I scrambled in, grabbed a couple bread rolls, and ran back outside. I handed each of the girls a piece of bread to thank them, which they hesitantly took and backed away bashfully. Selam nodded her approval, grabbed her water jug, and stepped toward her compound.

I started bringing my water inside when she called me, using the relaxed abbreviation of my Amharic name, "Solli!"

"*Abet?*" I replied, "Yeah?"

"Who am I?" She asked, awkwardly straddled the jug like I had done.

Woman filling up empty oil jugs with water from a seasonal spring.

I laughed and feigned ignorance, "Who?"

"You!"

We both laughed until we couldn't breathe, thrilled to share a joke without a language barrier. Once the laughing tapered off, I sternly stood up straight, formally wished Selam a good day—and pretended to spur the water jug between my legs into a trot. She gave me a crisp salute, and we each rode our awkward, yellow donkeys into our neighboring gates.

Claire and I taught an English class for high school students in our landlord's living room during the rainy season. One class had to be cut short because the room started flooding. The students jumped into action to barricade the back door as I sprinted into the yard and trenched in front of the door to divert some of the rainfall. Despite our best efforts, we still had to slosh through about four inches of water for the rest of class. We worked with the students to list and rank some of the issues that limited their access to education. The shortage of water, and potable water specifically, was the highest ranked problem for the students.

Debark gets its water from an open reservoir. The city-owned pipeline from the reservoir is prohibitively expensive for many people, vulnerable to breaks and contamination, and usually operational for only about two to three hours a week. These issues are a major problem for residents and visitors alike. Many local hotels lack sufficient storage for the water needed for park visitors. The price for lodging remains the same regardless of power and water availability, which is a common cause of

Claire celebrating the end of the rainy season with English class students.

complaint from tourists. The prevalence of water-borne illnesses is also a concern for residents and visitors. I only had to buy water from a neighbor two other times while in Ethiopia, but both were during repairs to the tap on our compound and not from the town reservoir running dry or being full of sediment. To fill our jugs, I had to walk to a nearby hotel that a friend of ours managed. I tried paying, but he refused to take anything. In response, I ordered tea in the small lobby and left a hefty tip. He politely refused three times, as is expected, before pocketing the small bills with a genuine smile.

However, many people in our part of town did not have the luxury of a tap in their own compound, which was shared with other families. They instead had to use public taps or overpay to use private taps, like Selam and I had done. They also didn't have the benefit of being a white ferenj who could afford to eat at a friend's hotel on a weekly basis. Even our modest living stipend as Volunteers was several times more than what these families earned from their physically demanding wage labor.

One day, a couple of girls who I would guess were seven years old, but likely much older, came to the compound asking to fill up three dirty and dented half-a-gallon plastic bottles. If they were coming to our compound for water that meant one of two things, they either didn't know we lived there, which was very unlikely, or they were desperate. The lack of surprise on their faces told me it was probably the second. They held out their bottles and 15 cents in birr coins—this was worth 8/10s of a cent, not even a penny. I reached out to the girl holding the coins and gently folded her fingers shut over them. I shook my head.

With no emotion, the girls dropped their arms and turned away, assuming I was not going to give them water. I caught them off guard when I told them to wait while I checked if our tap was flowing. It was, and I happily invited the girls inside. They were understandably cautious, but thankfully the tap was in the very front of the compound and they could see it through the large gaps in the fence. I told them to fill their bottles. They did and tried again to pay me. I made it clear I would not accept their coins and playfully shooed them out the gate.

I made it less than halfway back to our house when I heard someone shouting my name in the long-traveling sing-song speech common in the mountains. "Solomon! Sol-o-mon. Sol-o-mon!" I returned to the gate by the time the third "Sol—" had started and was met with a group of eight excited children, each holding an empty bottle. The boy in front who had called my name, I recognized as a local gumboy, a skilled hustler who sold individual sticks of chewing gum and packs of cheap cookies to travelers for a significant markup. He always accepted my first refusal to buy gum when I didn't want any. So, I made sure to buy from him whenever I did want a piece. He had a sixth sense for making a sale and would often appear with a shiny fan of my favorite gum flavors arranged on his wooden tray.

Like many neighborhood boys, I never heard his real name because he was called by his street name Abi. Only his family would call him by his real name. I asked Abi what they were doing, and he responded that they needed water too. I was equally alarmed and impressed by how quickly word had spread in the two minutes since the girls had left with their full bottles. I did not want to seem unfair, so I let the children inside to fill their bottles.

The tap ran on for the next 75 minutes. Bottle after bottle was swapped out for a new empty one. Were they bringing new bottles, or were they running home to empty them into a bigger jug and returning for more? The kids kept one eye on the bottles as they filled, and the other on me as I sat on the stoop of our landlord's house above them—a ferenj gargoyle observing them work. As children steadily flowed to the tap and back out again, I glanced at my indestructible, black brick of a phone which kept excellent time. I still had trouble believing how long this procession had been going on for.

I stood slowly, not wanting to spook the children, as if they were anxious animals drinking from a pond. The tap's blue metal handle came down with a clank, abruptly ending the static *whoosh* of flowing water that had filled our ears for over an hour. The children stared at me. And I stared back, not sure how to appropriately get them to leave. I made a slow chopping motion with my hand to say that was enough water. They accepted without complaint. There were no requests for more or arguments that some had taken more than others. The tap was now off, just as definitively as if it had stopped raining. The children thanked me and left without another word.

My generosity racked up an almost unheard-of water bill. The roughly 27-dollar bill for the month may have seemed reasonable, but not when water was only on for a few hours each week and the average income in town was about 1.5 dollars per day. Having a tap in the front of our compound was already a luxury, but I might as well have opened a public pool and water slide with that much water. Our landlord, who was also an excellent friend, always included water in our rent, but not this time. He asked that I go to the government office and pay the bill in full, in person. This may have been intended as a lesson in water use, but also a demonstration to the government that it was the foreigner using that much water—not him. As a respected and relatively affluent local, he understandably needed to be careful with how things appeared. He was also likely a little annoyed about a large water bill. In any case, a lesson was learned, and the tap stayed off. It was worth it.

ON HOLIDAY

*"It is no use walking anywhere to
preach unless our walking is our preaching."*
—Saint Francis of Assisi

*"To get away from one's working environment is,
in a sense, to get away from one's self; and this is often
the chief advantage of travel and change."*
—Charles Horton Cooley

Living and working in a foreign country is difficult. It is especially difficult when impersonal—or personal—attacks on your mental and physical health push you to a breaking point. Serving as a PCV is challenging. Individual challenges can last seconds, such as drive-by harassment from a child riding a donkey; can last months, such as the dry season; or even last years, such as navigating cultural differences. These challenges are often compounded by facing them alone. As Blaise Pascal wrote, "All men's miseries derive from not being able to sit in a quiet room alone." Even for couples serving together, as we were, Peace Corps can be a very isolating experience.

Volunteers so often confuse masochism with altruism. Like old fashioned remedies that in fact make things worse (think butter smeared on a burn), Volunteers know they are working because they hurt. Burnout is a sign of success. The only change worth pursuing comes from sweeping, grandiose projects. The anxiety to create and conduct these projects is as unwarranted as it is common among PCVs. It is important for Volunteers to find appropriate ways to rest and refill their metaphorical cups. Often, those cups aren't just metaphorical. One Volunteer from our conservation cohort introduced a local bar to the Black and Tan, a layered beer of pale ale and stout popular in parts of the USA. Dubbed the "striped hyena," this drink was a questionable example of the Peace Corps' second goal—bringing America to the world. However, it did demonstrate alcohol's ability to bridge cultural divides.

Volunteers develop their own coping strategies for living abroad. An outside observer may call these vices instead of strategies. They may seem more like escapism and avoidance as opposed to healthy outlets. Although tempting to judge the actions of Volunteers in such high-stress environments, doing so fails to recognize the sacrifices Volunteers make. That doesn't mean excusing behavior that puts them or others at risk, it

Derek playing foosball on the street with friends.

means realizing those decisions are theirs to make. Occasional pirated movie marathons, heavy drinking, and binge-eating Babybel cheese from care packages are excusable. Joining a rebel militia or riding a bicycle without a helmet are not.

Claire and I would periodically go to Gondar for urban amenities. Gondar is home to Dashen Brewery, which had surprisingly good beer and food. The brewery grounds were parklike, and you could spend hours talking, drinking, and eating. Some Volunteers and expat friends once spent 12 hours straight at the brewery. Beer is sold by the yard in a three-foot tall plexiglass cylinder with a tap at the bottom. Our group drank at least a football field worth of beer that day. Claire and I certainly enjoyed the brewery, but our trips to Gondar were primarily to take a hot shower (if the power was on) and stock up on a locally made cheese that could be kept unrefrigerated as long as you stayed on top of cutting off the mold. The beer, cheese, and (occasional) hot water were very welcome, but we especially looked forward to our infrequent trips to the truly urban capital, Addis Ababa.

In Ethiopia, all roads lead to Addis. The city was founded as the modern capital of Ethiopia in 1887 when, after a cold snap in the former mountainside capital of Entoto, Emperor Menelik II decided to move his headquarters closer to natural hot springs. These springs, called *filwuha* in Amharic, were a favorite leisure spot for the emperor and his wife Empress Taitu (Taytu). It was the empress who, being as shrewd a marketer as she was a stateswoman, named the city "New Flower."

Emperor Haile Selassie developed the hot springs as a public bathhouse during his rule. The bathhouse was outdated while we lived in Ethiopia—and still is—but made for a singular Ethiopian experience. We were encouraged to go to the bathhouse by a friend who managed the Simien Lodge inside the park. As someone who successfully maintained a high-class image in rural Ethiopia, we trusted her recommendation. That was a mistake, but not one I regret.

The bathhouse was composed of several brutalist, concrete buildings with dome skylights covering the roofs like warts on a toad, while the interior was bright and well-ventilated by massive shutters. The baths were divided into numerous public and private areas, both single-gender and mixed. As instructed by our high-class friend, we had paid for individual bathing treatments, so we waited in a small public pool for our allotted times—one of the only things in Ethiopia that operated on a strict schedule. Bathing suits were required in all but the individual treatment rooms, where one was expected to be nude to be sufficiently "treated." When my time had arrived, I was escorted to a large room divided by opaque plastic sheets. It was filled with steam and the heady smell of boiling mineral water and body odor. My attendant, a middle-aged Ethiopian with dark skin and a white mustache, pulled aside one of the sheets and led me into a smaller room walled in by the plastic. In the middle of the room was what could only be described as a giant porcelain wok.

As directed, I took off my bathing suit and awkwardly sat cross-legged in the middle of the wok…bathtub…spa. The attendant never gave me his name, which was unusual coming from a rural market town where people volunteered their names almost immediately. He was understandably uninterested in introducing himself to naked ferenjis. He cleared his throat and turned a knob to start the flow of water into the tub. I waited as the water rose past my navel and watched while the attendant untangled a length of plastic tubing on the floor. It was roughly one inch in diameter and had a sun-cracked plastic nozzle at its tip. If this were a science fiction movie, the audience would have been screaming at me to RUN!

The attendant mimed for me to lay down in my personal cooking vessel as he brought the tubing to the edge. I complied. He turned another knob, and a powerful jet of warm water shot from the nozzle. The tub was deep enough for me to lay mostly covered by water—except for my head and feet which were held up by the curved sides of the spa. I let my hands float casually over my groin, wanting to cover myself while not looking like a prude American. The man gave me a passive thumbs up in approval and began massaging my legs with the high-powered water jet. He continued power washing my body above and below the water surface. I alternated feeling like a pale potato being boiled for stew and a gangly baby giraffe getting sprayed down against its will.

Did it feel good? *Yes.* Was it exceptionally, excruciatingly awkward? *Also, yes.* Peace Corps in a nutshell.

Volunteers unable or unwilling to address their health are often forced to leave the country, willingly or unwillingly. One member of our group left only a few weeks after arriving, during our pre-service training. He had called the Peace Corps office and asked to leave. He was on the next flight home before anyone knew he was gone. Another member left after a year. He felt he wasn't making any progress at his site and was just surviving. He had struggled through the first year, and his decision to leave was not a surprise. One Volunteer left with just a few months remaining before completing his service. He was offered a job that he couldn't decline. These voluntary removals are called Early Termination (ET) and are treated like a resignation.

However, some Volunteers are told to leave. This may be for health reasons known as Medical Separation (MS)—medical issues that cannot be effectively treated in country, including mental health emergencies. MS was discussed when I was slammed against the ceiling of a public bus when it hit a bump. The bus didn't have functioning shocks, and I was sitting in the very last row. A 50-dollar MRI scan taken in the basement of a strip mall in Addis Ababa showed severe inflammation but no permanent damage.

Peace Corps makes Volunteers identify the closest spot where a plane or helicopter could set down to evacuate them if needed. One member of our group was airlifted from his site by US Air Force personnel due to severe abdominal pain. It thankfully ended up being a minor issue. But it drove home the point that these evacuations weren't just a hypothetical need. Another group member was flown to a hospital in South Africa due to a condition called *Acanthamoeba keratitis*. This meant amoebas hitched a ride on a contact lens and began eating his eye. Luckily, the hospital was able to treat it, and the Volunteer returned after a few weeks. He did develop a permanent blurry dot in his vision and was given the option to be Medically Separated, but he decided to stay. In general, Peace Corps takes the healthcare of its Volunteers very seriously. Some countries are better or worse in this regard, but most country staff realize that neglecting an injured Volunteer reflects poorly on them and the country overall. The medical staff in Ethiopia were reliable and empathetic. We were fortunate.

Volunteers can also be "dishonorably discharged," called Administrative Separation (AS), or Admin Sep for short. This amounts to being fired from the Peace Corps. It is neither rare nor common. It is the reality of some people being unsuited to Peace Corps service, due to poor decision-making or just bad luck. One woman from our group was Administratively Separated. She had a reputation in her community for partying and was away from her site for weeks at a time. She became increasingly incapable of caring for herself, and other Volunteers urged the Peace Corps medical office to act. She was directed to have a psychiatric consultation at the Peace Corps head office in Washington DC when she flew home for the holidays. If cleared by medical staff there, she would have been allowed to return to Ethiopia. Otherwise, she would have to be Medically Separated. She wasn't cleared to return to Ethiopia but did anyway. She was Administratively Separated as soon as the Peace Corps Ethiopia staff knew she was back. Instead of being Medically Separated, she was fired, eliminating any chance of serving in the Peace Corps again.

Most cases of Admin Sep aren't so dramatic. It is most common when Volunteers behave badly, break rules intended to keep them safe, and/or break host country laws. Volunteers in a different program area, yet serving at the same time, were separated because they smoked cannabis while in service. Despite Ethiopian Emperor Haile Selassie being the literal messiah for Rastafarians, marijuana is illegal in Ethiopia. A strong black market for marijuana still exists, and it is not difficult to find, especially among younger Ethiopians. Peace Corps staff became aware of the group smoking and questioned them. The Volunteers admitted to it and were flown home shortly thereafter. This was a very unpopular decision because the Volunteers were only a couple of months away from completing their service.

A successful Close of Service (COS) would have given them the federal hiring benefits and personal accomplishment of finishing their 27 months of service. That opportunity was taken away to protect the Volunteers from potential jail time in an Ethiopian prison and to prevent Peace Corps Ethiopia from getting a diplomatic black eye. It still stung though. Successfully completing Peace Corps service to become a Returned Peace Corps Volunteer (RPCV) is a minor distinction, but one that Volunteers are rightfully very proud of.

STREET DOG

"He who is cruel to animals becomes hard also in his dealings with men. We can judge the heart of a man by his treatment of animals."

—Immanuel Kant

"The greatness of a nation can be judged by the way its animals are treated."

—Mahatma Gandhi

When Claire and I moved to Debark from inside the park, there was a mother dog with several puppies on our fenced compound. She was very sweet, and we started putting out water for her, which led to putting out food, which led to belly rubs. We were asked so often whose dog she was until one day it just made sense to say she was ours. We called her Mama Dog and were later told that her Amharic name was Titi, which literally means "mama." Although Titi is the locally ubiquitous name for any female dog that is old enough to breed, this Titi was special—at least to us. Despite being harassed, beaten, stoned, and yelled at daily, she was still capable of loving a person. Because people in our area had gotten used to Titi, and because she took care of the unwanted animal byproducts that resulted from slaughtering livestock, she was allowed to stay.

The father of some of the puppies, Jibbe, meaning "my hyena," was also on the compound much of the time. He was an excellent though excitable guard dog. He wouldn't allow anyone he didn't know into the compound. The thick-headed dog finally understood that he didn't need to bark at everything when, after several sleepless nights, I broke a plate over his head. It was a cheap plastic plate, but it still got the message across. He was more selective with his late-night alarms. Despite his disagreeable nature, Jibbe was superb with the puppies and particularly enjoyed playing with the female puppy that looked exactly like him. About two months after he started trusting us and greeting us when we came onto the compound, he was attacked by the dog of the previous Volunteer in Debark and died from his wounds.

    Tankara, meaning "strong one," was massive, aggressive, and deserving of his nickname, Tank. Shortly after killing Jibbe, Tank was killed by poison put out by the local government to deal with feral dogs, and we admittedly felt relieved. Tank would come into our compound and start fights, or walk right into our house and snap at us when we made him leave. I felt guilty thinking that Debark was safer with him dead, but neighbors and I were fed up with his constant aggression. I felt bad that his owner had disappeared when he left Ethiopia, but that was no excuse for trying to bite what he didn't like, which was everything that moved.

    Without the drama of Jibbe and Tankara, that left just Mama Dog and her puppies. One by one the puppies were rounded up and taken away. The males would be given away or sold to people to use as guard dogs, and the females were likely killed or abandoned outside of Debark. There was one puppy that would not let anyone within ten feet of her. She took her father's distrust of humans to the extreme. Whenever she saw a person, she would yelp like she was being kicked and retreat while looking over her shoulder. No one could get close enough to her to catch her, so she stayed. With some help from her mother, she learned we would not harm her. We could also miraculously make bread appear from our pockets.

She became our constant companion after several months. Wherever we were, we could count on her being in our shadow. She would follow us to the bus station whenever we left town and would wait just outside the bus door for as long as it took for the bus to fill up and leave, which often took 1–3 hours. She would then trot back to the compound, having completed her mission to protect us. She had a beautiful earthy-red coat and a pointed snout from her ancestry of hybridization between Ethiopian wolves and the pedigreed dogs left behind by Italian officers during WWII. She got her color and self-assuredness from her father, but her temperament and love of human affection all came from her mother. We named her Ambasha, after the light, reddish brown bread that was cut into wedges and often served with coffee. We called her Basha for short, which we later learned was the title for low-ranking government officials. This became a gold mine for inappropriate jokes.

Basha following us everywhere sometimes caused problems; usually when around Muslims who believed dogs were unclean, and when visiting government offices. Once while waiting to speak with the park warden, Basha marched right into the warden's office to announce that he was wasting our time. Basha, Claire, and I all received a lecture about how inappropriate it was for a dog to be in a building. Despite such cultural duties to dislike dogs, Basha became somewhat of a celebrity in town, and we got offers from people willing to buy her, or at least take her when we went to the market. I began writing a foolhardy grant proposal to take Basha back to America with us. As an Ethiopian wolf hybrid, we planned to take her to schools or other organizations to discuss the rarest canid on Earth. Despite the wolf's charisma and its highly endangered status, very few Americans have heard of the species. We thought it would be a great opportunity to bring a beloved Ethiopian family member back with us and to hopefully get Americans more involved in protecting a flagship species on the brink of extinction.

We were looking forward to the end of the rainy season and hopefully getting more work to do as the tourist season approached. Titi had yet another litter of puppies, and Basha became the perfect big sister. She would play with them, clean up after them, and let them sleep in a pile on her back when the chilly rains sucked the heat out of the world. In August, Basha developed what appeared to have been an eye infection, and rings of crust formed on her eyelids. This occasionally forced her

Basha sitting with puppies by the outhouse.

eyes shut, and she became very lethargic. We were starting to get worried when the infection seemed to improve on its own and she began playing with her younger siblings again. But things got much worse for Basha. Her nose became dry, hot, and caked with mucus. She still played with her siblings and followed us around town but had trouble breathing.

Eventually, she stopped playing, stopped being our shadow, and ultimately stopped eating. The mucus streamed down her nose turned into a red gunk, and she stopped drinking. We mixed milk in with her water to try to get her some nutrition, but she stumbled away as fast as she could, acting as if we had swatted her on the face. The fear of water was a worrying symptom of rabies, and we grew even more anxious. There is no known cure for an active, symptomatic rabies infection—making it a painful death sentence for dogs and humans. Only one PCV in Ethiopia has died during their service. He was just 27 and died from rabies despite being flown to medical facilities outside the country.

After two days, Basha's hoarse bark sounded more like an arthritic old hound instead of a puppy less than a year old. She could no longer focus her eyes, snapping at shadows and yelping at imaginary people. She couldn't even stand on her own. She spent two days only being able to lie down, bicycle kicking and tearing at the ground with the side of her mouth. Mud and grass caked over her teeth and plastered her palate. We let ourselves cry that night and wondered if she would be dead in the morning. After almost a week of suffering, it would have been a relief to both her and us if she did not wake up.

We awoke to the sound of rain on our tin roof and Basha's hoarse, mournful howl. We went outside to find her soaking wet, her fur plastered to her body, trying to crawl up against the wall of the house to get out of the rain. She was not more than three feet from where we had seen her lying before, and it had rained throughout the night. Not being able to see or smell well, she half-heartedly snapped at us as we pushed her up to a dry spot and covered her in a thin blanket. There was nothing more we could do, so we went back inside and tried to distract ourselves by reading. It worked, but not well. The rain picked up, and our bedroom became the inside of a drum as hail and rain battered the corrugated steel roof. A gurgling howl set our teeth on edge, breaking through the rattling hail's call-to-arms. We had almost, just almost, forgotten what we were distracting ourselves from.

 I ran over to the window, unlatched the bolt, and pulled it open as fast as I could. My heart broke, and I choked off a "God dammit" as I looked out. In the hours since we last saw her, Basha had crawled across most of the compound yard to get to the outhouse where it was relatively dry and warm. Like most Ethiopian *chika bet* (buildings made of mud, straw, and wood poles), the outhouse had a stone foundation. That, combined with the slight slope the compound was built on, created a two-foot-tall wall between ground level and the wooden outhouse door. Basha was lying in a puddle of mud, water, and accumulated hail just at the base of this ledge. From the way she was sprawled in the puddle, it was clear that she had tried to get into the doorway, failed, and fallen into the puddle growing at the base of the foundation. She was trying to stand up, but after her exhausting crawl across the compound she could only lift her head a few inches and slap it back down. It was one of the worst sights of my life. She was a good dog. A dog that was now exhausted and half-drowned in a three-inch puddle of freezing water and mud.

 I ran out of the house and grabbed one of the blankets she liked to sleep on from inside the outhouse. I had forgotten to put on a raincoat, but by the time I realized, it didn't matter. The water was running down my clothes in sheets when I reached her. I wrapped the blanket around her. My first thought was to warm her; but, I twisted the blanket into a crude sling to avoid her poorly directed bites and make it easier to lift her out of the puddle. I pushed her through the open doorway and into the dry building. In a moment of lucidity, she seemed to understand I was trying to help her, stopped snapping, and scrambled up the ledge as best she could. I set the writhing bundle on the mud floor and wrapped the blanket around her, trying to dry her as I tucked the blanket edges under.

I stood and looked toward the window through which I had first spotted her and saw Claire looking back at me. "She is dying," I said, mostly to myself, but Claire's slow nod told me that she had been strong enough to comprehend that before I had. Claire came out, and we both stayed in the outhouse with Basha for a while, but we left when we realized that we couldn't do anything more for her. We checked on her several times an hour, and there was no improvement aside from her drying off, her fever warming her from the inside out.

That night, our neighbor Selam came to say hello because she had just gotten back from an extended visit to Dabat. She asked how we were, but we couldn't hide that something was wrong, especially since she stopped by just as I was going to check on Basha. I opened the outhouse door and motioned inside. Selam gasped when she saw Basha's heaving chest. She had rolled out of the blanket and was restlessly biting the mud floor. The mud was caked so thick on the roof of her mouth that she couldn't even pull her tongue all the way back into her mouth.

Selam cooed and slowly turned back to face me. "She is defeated," she said in English. She shook her head and continued in Amharic, "She was a very beautiful dog." Selam had called our

Mother and daughter, Titi (left) and Basha (right).

dogs *konjo* (beautiful) before, but this time she had used the past tense. She meant, "She had been a very beautiful dog." Basha was already dead. Her body just hadn't caught up with reality yet—and neither had we. Selam told me about a man who would come and put down sick animals, but since it was a Sunday evening, he would not be available until the next day. I understood her Amharic, but coldly played dumb because I still didn't want to admit that having a stranger come and put down our dog was a valid option. Paying someone to haphazardly bludgeon our dog to death wasn't a mercy killing in my mind.

There is a cliff in the park ominously named Cuchella Motaya. The name is loosely interpreted as "the place where puppies die." Veterinary services, especially spaying and neutering, are nonexistent in the park. Even if park occupants can afford to bait dogs with poisoned meat, as is done in urban areas, they are not allowed because wildlife would be killed as well. Instead, unwanted puppies are dropped off the cliff to quickly end their lives before they open their eyes. What I first thought as cruel and detached now seemed to be an act of kindness. An uncontrolled dog population in the park would not be positive for the dogs, their owners, park visitors, or resident wildlife. Selam left as Claire and I weighed our options: leave Basha in the outhouse until her lungs filled with fluid and she stopped breathing, hire someone to put her down the next day at the earliest, or put her down ourselves that night. After more than an hour of pacing and cursing, we came to what we knew was the best decision for us and Basha. The dog that helped us stay in Ethiopia after failed projects with the national park, the dog that we had already committed to take home with us, was about to be put down on a mud outhouse floor with a rock.

THE UGLY ROCK

"Heartbreak is life educating us."
—George Bernard Shaw

"Before you know kindness as the deepest thing inside, you must know sorrow as the other deepest thing."
—Naomi Shihab Nye

Basha deserved much better, but it was the best we could give her. Despite Claire's offer to do it, there was no way I would feel comfortable waiting outside while she put her down. Even with salt-crusted eyes, I was set on doing it myself. I asked Claire—knelt on the outhouse floor—to say one last goodby. Basha turned, yelping and nipping. There was nothing Claire could do except stand and leave. Our puppy was already gone.

I selected a grapefruit-sized rock that had once been part of the house's foundation before the rain rotted the mortar holding it in place, walked into the outhouse, and shut the door behind me. I didn't want to see what I was doing, let alone have anyone else see. This was the right thing to do, but I was ashamed to do it. I slowly crouched and patted her side, being careful to avoid her pointed, coyote-like snout. She swung her head to bite, but I rested my hand just out of reach of her teeth and close enough to her blood crusted nose for her to smell me. She calmed and rested her head back on the floor, letting out a deep breath and a high-pitched whine. Her cheeks pulled in with each breath, and her ribs seemed to jump against the skin. I stroked her head and said I was sorry.

I looked at the rock in my hand and hefted its weight. What an ugly fucking rock. I slammed the rock down as hard as I could, dimpling the floor and startling Basha. I made another practice swing into the floor and then went through the motions just above Basha's half-closed eye. I willed the rock to bring itself down. Pushing the rock as hard as I could, I bored into it with my eyes. It refused to move. Suddenly, without warning and without any conscious thought of my own, the rock seemed to feel my impatient desperation and came down on Basha's head. She yelped, weak and flat. The rain-softened dirt floor had absorbed more of the impact than I expected, and it would take more than one strike. I had to bring the rock down three more times, now under my own willpower, before her staccato yelps stopped.

Basha's body relaxed, and her tense legs settled at her side. I knelt, frozen. Her chest didn't move again until she let out a final slow exhale. I broke. Leaning against the door, I tried to stand but only slid down it to the floor. I cried until my hands shook, my head throbbed, and my vision narrowed to pinpricks of color at the end of blinding white tunnels.

Claire called for me from the other side of the door. Her distant voice told me that she loved me and that I needed to come outside. I gradually came back to my senses as my breath slowed and the white tunnels retracted back into my head. I felt drained and fundamentally changed, like a sea leached of the salt that defined it. The water was still there, filling the cracks of the earth and disguising sunken mountains with the illusion of calm waves. But it looked wrong, sounded wrong, felt...wrong.

I noticed a drop of blood on the floor and assumed it was Basha's. But when I looked at her there was no sign of blood anywhere. As Claire and I first talked about what we had to do, I kept picturing an expanding, dark red halo around Basha's head. This grim tableau was fed by years of action movies and gory TV shows. I felt a drop of something roll down my spine and glanced at the door. The crude nails holding a tin sheet to the door's wood frame were sticking out and had grazed my back as I slid to the floor. It was only a scratch, but the blood somehow made what had happened more real. I got up, opened the door, and went out, anxious for the next step to be over with.

It wasn't long before Claire and I were standing over Basha's motionless body with a food aid grain sack in our hands. We knelt one last time and said our goodbyes. I lifted her as dignified as I could, but her limp body seemed to fight my attempt to put her in the sack. Eventually, we were able to lower her into the bag and curl her body, as if she was sleeping with her head resting on her front paws. We tied the sack shut, carried her to the storage room that shared a wall with the outhouse, and covered the sac with multiple blankets to protect the body as best we could from rats.

The moon had come up while we were moving the body, and most of Debark, except for a party at a local hotel, had closed its doors. We watched a movie on our laptop for the sake of normalcy and eventually fell asleep. We woke up the next morning, and neither of us wanted to say anything just in case it had not happened. The reality was that I had stoned our dog to death the night before and her body was stiffening in the storeroom.

Once we couldn't deny what had happened any longer, I walked to the local kebele office to see if we needed to do something with the body because she had been sick, and ran into our good friend Misgano. He had known Basha was very sick and was extremely sorry to hear that she was gone. Misgano, ever the caring and helpful neighbor, offered to take care of Basha's body for us. He and his friend Gebre followed me back to our compound where they both picked up a corner of the sack. They awkwardly stepped out of the compound with the bag slung between them. Later that morning, they came back to let us know what they had done. Basha was buried in a shallow grave on the edge of town in a eucalyptus plantation.

Following Basha's death, we were consoled by the six energetic puppies in the compound and redirected our attention to them and their mother. Titi, the canine matriarch, had found herself a new "husband" after Jibbe's death. Our 11-year-old neighbor had informed us that they were, in fact, married. Not realizing that he would be around far longer than Jibbe, we had given him the highly unimaginative name of Tikuru, literally meaning "the black one." Over the next two months, four of the puppies were given away, sometimes multiple times because they made their way back to our compound. There were two puppies left on the compound along with their newlywed parents.

Derek walking over a drainage with Tikuru close behind.

The male puppy was meant to stay on the compound to become a guard dog. The female puppy had inherited and even improved on her mother's friendliness. We wouldn't allow anyone to take her away in a plastic bag, as most dogs are transported in Ethiopia. We planned on getting her spayed at the veterinary school in Gondar and then finding a home for her with someone we trusted. In October, we traveled to the Bale Mountains on the southern rim of the rift valley to do fieldwork with some researchers from Colorado State University. The work required us to be gone from Debark for almost a month. On our trip, we spent several days at Wondo Genet College of Forestry to give seminars, relax on the beautiful campus, and visit two other Volunteers who lived there.

We got a call from the Volunteer who lived at the scout camp near Limalimo Pass. He shared the awful news that both puppies had contracted the same disease that Basha had and were found dead outside a neighbor's house. Our long ride back to Debark was even longer than usual. It was clear once we arrived that those two puppies were not the only victims of the disease. All the puppies from their litter had died—all of them. Dogs all over town had slowly succumbed to the illness as it spread over several weeks. We eventually concluded that the disease was either canine influenza or distemper. Many locals went to witch doctors to buy cultural medicines to protect themselves. We tried telling people that humans couldn't get sick from either disease, but tradition won out and people still shelled out money for bitter, ineffectual concoctions.

The perpetual fear of rabies demanded action, even if it accomplished nothing except for the feeling of being proactive. There had not been an outbreak in Debark for almost ten years, but people expected every dog to be a potential carrier. It is possible for people to contract the distemper virus, yet it doesn't cause serious illness. Rabies, however, is quite possibly the worst disease a human can die from—gradually losing one's mind and dying from dehydration as it ravishes the brain over days. Contracting rabies is nearly always a death sentence, unless a special course of vaccines can be given immediately after exposure.

I was fortunate to have access to these medical treatments when I was bitten by a loose guard dog on the way home from the market one day. The dog didn't show any signs of rabies, but I was medically evacuated to the Peace Corps medical office in Addis Ababa just to be safe. I had to stay for a week to receive the required series of injections. Exceptionally few Ethiopians can fly to the capital city with less than a day's notice, let alone stay in a hotel for a week so they can get the time-sensitive medication.

The point of sharing this experience is not to make people sad. Sadness for the sake of sadness is the worst possible entertainment. I'm not advocating for a "Simien Mountains Animal Sanctuary" or for funding to spay and neuter Ethiopian street dogs. Both would have value to animals and humans, but the human need is too great. However, diseases that are transmissible between humans and animals need more attention in international work. Roughly 60% of human diseases originate in animals and then spread through close contact. Purely human issues receive massive amounts of funding thrown at them, and people rarely stop to ask if the money can be better spent on other issues. HIV/AIDS is an excellent example.

The Human Immunodeficiency Virus (HIV) is the virus

responsible for causing Acquired Immunodeficiency Syndrome (AIDS). Genetic analysis has shown that HIV likely originated when a hunter or bushmeat vendor was bitten or cut when handling an animal infected with a Simian Immunodeficiency Virus (SIV). Once a classic example of a zoonotic disease—disease spread between animals and humans—that jumped from primates to humans, HIV became a moral dilemma. It became an issue when it started jumping oceans and was recognized in the early 1980s as a "first-world problem," not just a problem in developing countries. Zoonotic diseases and diseases that afflict domestic animals or wildlife, need more attention before they become threats to human survival. This is even more important following the COVID-19 pandemic, an alarming case study of viruses spreading from animals, likely bats in this case, to humans.

Billions of dollars are still being spent on public health programs with only marginal benefits because the same work has been done for years. Cultural norms and traditions can also create an uphill battle for public health issues. I was told more than once in Ethiopia that drinking water from a river blessed on the Timket holiday, or sleeping with a virgin, or eating enormous quantities of ginger could cure AIDS. These activities will not cure AIDS, but they may infect an innocent person with HIV, give someone a parasite, and may lead to low blood pressure and thin blood, respectively. Well-meaning and well-funded public health campaigns can be derailed by such objectively harmful traditional practices. Such practices should be recognized and challenged, but their influences cannot be ignored for funding to have the desired health outcomes.

Even if such effort-based programs improve the quality of life for select program recipients, they risk becoming background noise that doesn't result in continual improvements or lasting changes. Targeted, goal-based programs with clearly communicated funding windows can build capacity without creating dependency on foreign aid. Goal setting and program development will still take years to become sustainable, but funding is not open-ended. Wealthier nations want to help, yet citizens rely largely on political agendas set by their governments. Having seen and heard how several international aid organizations spend money, I cannot support those that exist primarily for their own continued existence.

The amount spent on legitimate change and improvement is objectively massive, yet relatively minuscule when compared to the total amount given by foreign benefactors. Immense overhead costs and the involvement of jet-setting "experts" from developed nations can sap funds, but these are often treated as just the cost of doing business in the global south. Shiny, white 4x4 vehicles paid for by international governments or NGOs, chauffeur shiny, (usually) white saviors on poverty safaris, visiting project sites and "maintaining a presence in project communities." A few success stories for public outreach brochures and donor reports are good enough to keep the lights on and vehicles fueled.

For centuries, people have noticed that the way someone treats animals is often an indicator of how they treat other humans. The Latin root of the word "compassion" means "to suffer with." I have some wonderful friends but have never had a friend willing to suffer with me as much as dogs have. Before you write me off as some crazy misanthrope who hoards animals in my living room, I admit I was once disgusted by the amount of money people donate to animal causes instead of human ones.

After two years of witnessing daily animal abuse and the impact this has on people, I can say that animal welfare is both an ethical and practical dilemma that deserves more attention. I have spent the last two decades of my life picking apart these issues in both personal and academic settings. The bitter truth is that most human problems are caused by human failures. In many cases, these failures occur in the countries where these problems are found. Attempts to solve these failures using mostly foreign funds and expertise can result in deep-rooted feelings of dependency and inadequacy. These solutions may be short-lived because they are neither culturally appropriate nor sustainable without constant donor funds.

On the other hand, animal welfare projects in developing nations help those that are truly helpless and victims of the environment around them. Such projects can improve longevity and quality of life for humans and animals alike. It is also less likely that international involvement will develop into a culture of dependency because people benefit from these projects indirectly through

Faculty at the veterinary school in Gondar conducting a health exam for dogs.

improved agricultural production and lower risks of disease. Dr. Giuseppe Bertoni, Italian professor emeritus at Zootechnics, has demonstrated through his research that healthy animals result in a safer food supply, higher farm productivity (including an increased number of offspring), reduced environmental impact, reduced use of antibiotics, and improved animal welfare. Rabies prevention and vaccination programs are an excellent example of this because rabies can be equally deadly for humans, livestock, and wildlife.

I am not ignoring the reality of life in developing countries or the hardships that humans face. I am saying that there is a tremendous need that is not being met by the current cumbersome system of international aid. Animals have the distinct advantage and disadvantage of not being politicians. They cannot advocate for themselves.

AWFULLY GOOD. TERRIBLY FANTASTIC. PRETTY UGLY.

"Let me never fall into the vulgar mistake of dreaming that I am persecuted whenever I am contradicted."
—Ralph Waldo Emerson

"I believe that truth has only one face: that of a violent contradiction."
—Georges Bataille

By now, you may be able to tell I am drawn toward the melancholic, melodramatic, and the occasionally macabre. I gravitate toward philosophies like Greek stoicism and Japanese *wabi sabi,* despite having never visited either country. I particularly like unfiltered beer, despite getting a hangover after just one. I sometimes find goodness in what other people find ascetic, crude, or in bad taste. It can be difficult to say that something is definitively good or bad. Who is something good or bad for? What outcome is desirable or undesirable? Such legalistic, black-and-white labels do not, and cannot, portray the full reality.

Of course, there are objectively terrible or wonderful events that cause undeniable harm or benefit. I'm not arguing that everything happens on an ethical grayscale. Black and white do exist. However, reality cannot be found in the middle through a compromise of the two—a watering down. It can be found through a kind of holistic ambivalence, an aggregation of both the terribly fantastic and the fantastically terrible. Just as the average of an astronomically large number and an infinitesimally small number results in a meaningless point in between, the averaging of an experience often results in a meaningless phrase like, "It was interesting," or, "It was OK."

The only way I have found to adequately portray my experience as a PCV is with an oxymoron or otherwise contradictory statement. Peace Corps has been awful, and it has been good; it has been "awfully good." Ethiopia is pretty, and it is ugly; it is "pretty ugly." I never really appreciated phrases like "pretty ugly" until I came to Africa.

Camp GLOW (Girls Leading Our World) is a Peace Corps program meant to teach young women, and men, about gender equality and leading more fulfilling lives in general. As is tradition, we held a talent show on the last night of camp. Many campers exhibited their talents as singers, dancers, writers, and

Camp GLOW students from around the Amhara region.

comedians. One of the students told a joke about then Prime Minister Meles Zenawi which elicited as many gasps as guffaws. Some background is required to understand how dangerous yet warranted the joke was.

Human Rights Watch, an international human rights advocacy group, has questioned the Ethiopian government numerous times and published public reports on their findings. The previous Ethiopian government—before Prime Minister Abiy dissolved it in 2019—operated under an ideology it called "Revolutionary Democracy." The name packed lots of patriotic pizazz, but that's just good marketing. Meles was very clear about the intended result of this democracy:

> "When Revolutionary Democracy permeates the entire society, individuals will start to think alike, and all persons will cease having their own independent outlook. In this order, individual thinking becomes simply part of collective thinking because the individual will not be in a position to reflect on concepts that have not been proscribed by Revolutionary Democracy."

If this concept sounds familiar, it may be because it is almost verbatim from George Orwell's dystopian *1984*. It is Big Brother's ultimate plan to control the thoughts of its citizenry to the point where any dissentious thought cannot even be born in the first place. People cannot oppose the government because they cannot think to oppose the government.

For better and worse, Meles' government was often compared to the previous militaristic Derg regime. *Derg* means "council" in Amharic. This is an innocuous name for the government that overthrew Emperor Haile Selassie and launched the Red Terror that imprisoned and executed tens of thousands of political opponents. Our neighbor Selam expressed it the best way I could imagine when I asked her what she thought. She formed her hand into a pistol, placed it against my forehead, and pulled the trigger. The imaginary hammer of her thumb struck the imaginary bullet in her palm and sent it burrowing into my very real brain. "This is what the Derg was like," she said. Then, she stepped behind me, formed her hand into the same gun, and pulled the trigger. "I disappeared, however you still died."

The message was simple: When the Derg stepped up and put a bullet in your head, you saw it coming, but Meles shot you in the back. Despite ubiquitous propaganda, Meles Zenawi couldn't win the war of the minds, and I knew this because he had already lost. It was just a question of when the ruling party, the Ethiopian people, and the international community realized it. Here was the joke the student told at camp:

> Prime Minister Meles Zenawi is flying over Ethiopia in his private jet with some of his advisers. He looks out the airplane window and sees how sad and poor the Ethiopians below him are. He pulls a 100-birr [roughly 5 dollars at the time] bill out of his pocket and is about to throw it out of the plane when one of his advisers stops him.
> "Why are you throwing that 100-birr note out of the plane?" he asks.
> "Because I want to give someone 100 birr, and then they will be happy," Meles responds.
> "Then why don't you throw two 50-birr bills out of the plane and that way two people will be happy?"
> Meles is about to throw two bills when another adviser says, "You should throw ten 10-birr bills out of the plane so that ten people will get them and be happy."
> A third adviser stops him again and says, "No, you should throw one hundred 1-birr bills out of the plane and that way one hundred people will be happy."
> Meles thinks this is a good idea until he

turns to his last adviser. "Well, why don't you speak? What is your suggestion?"

The advisor stares at Meles and says, "You should throw yourself out of the plane and that way everyone in Ethiopia will be happy."

Meles was dead less than a month later, and all of Ethiopia was in mourning. Whether it was real or forced, Ethiopians all over the country wailed and gnashed their teeth. It was at least partially the result of the potent mix of centuries of Ethiopian culture and the government propaganda that completely dominated Ethiopian communications for weeks after the death. Even if Ethiopians do not know or even like the person who dies, they still mourn for them as a show of solidarity and respect, and in the hope that they will similarly be mourned at their own passing.

Ethiopia didn't mourn the African strongman and dictator who oversaw a pageant of democracy for decades. The country didn't mourn the man who imprisoned journalists for telling the truth, the man who forced people off their land to lease it to foreign governments, or the man who took billions of dollars from the Ethiopian people to build a controversial hydroelectric dam that neighboring countries cursed. Ethiopia mourned the liberator who saved them from the injustice and cruelty of the Derg. The country mourned the symbol of Ethiopian development and political hegemony on the African continent. There were numerous billboards and posters around Addis Ababa lamenting the fact that, "Africa has lost her one eye." Meles' rule was an expression of the Ethiopian desire for a better life, but also the unwillingness to accept the difficulties associated with that life. It is not easy to say whether Ethiopia developed because of Meles or despite him. Whichever opinion you choose, the death of Meles Zenawi was still awfully good.

Claire and I traveled to Bahir Dar for our COS conference. While reminiscing with our friends from our training group and planning our respective futures, we received one of the most enduring lessons of the awfully good. We were unaware about being taught such a lesson until we returned to our home in Debark. While we had been gone, someone had broken the window on our front door and pushed the glass into the house and onto the floor. Luckily, there were bars welded to the door which prevented the burglar from climbing through and stealing everything we owned. There was not much, but our treasure trove of care boxes and laboriously haggled local goods was what allowed us to function. The walls of the house were wattle and daub, with layers of clay and animal dung smeared between the wooden wattle of eucalyptus poles. This construction was surprisingly comfortable as it was strong.

However, it could not withstand the efforts of someone determined to get inside. The broken window was maddening, inconvenient, and insulting, but not threatening. But that was not the only evidence left at the scene of the crime. The icing on the doorstep was a freshly deposited, child-sized stool. Just to clarify, I don't mean an adorably miniature seat designed for young people. I mean a child took a child-sized shit just to the side of our front door. When I noticed (i.e., smelled) the present, I wasn't able to be angry. Honestly, I was not even a little surprised that it was there. Oh, an Ethiopian kid took a dump right outside our front door while we were gone? Of course they did. Why not? Why wouldn't an Ethiopian child do that in front of the ferenj's house? Such irrational games of cause and effect were not uncommon for foreigners, yet they generally weren't so difficult to clean without wasting precious water in the dry season.

What did surprise me, however, was the reaction of Gebre, the man who was watching our landlord's house while he was away. Gebre was younger than we were, but he had deep lines at the corners of his large, round eyes. The lines were evidence of the hours spent squinting in the sun as he worked his small farm plot to grow garlic. He was quick to smile, which further chiseled those same grooves to the point that dust would sometimes collect in them. The short man always wore a fleece blanket wrapped around him like a traditional Amharan gabi. Instead of the customary handwoven white cotton used in wraps widely worn by elders, the blanket was a cheap Chinese import with an elaborate design of gold filigree. Although intended to look fancy, it looked like a Victorian-era tablecloth only used at Christmas. Its unapologetic gaudiness suited Gebre well in an ironic sort of way—equally warm and vulgar.

Our house was in the same fenced compound as our landlord's. After our window was broken, Gebre slept on the floor of our outhouse for three nights because he was worried someone would come back and try to break in. Now, really think about that for a few seconds. Sleeping...outhouse floor...three nights. The outhouse where I put Basha down, where we showered with buckets warmed on a camp stove, where a plastic tote held used toilet paper to be burned later. A man we hardly knew beyond Amharic pleasantries slept on a pit latrine floor for three nights because he wanted our house to be safe. That was awfully good of him.

Peace Corps is not a tidy experience, and generalizations are nearly impossible to make about Volunteers' experiences in the same country, let alone different countries. The first several groups of Volunteers in Ethiopia had some of the highest resignation rates of any Peace Corps post. However, these groups also had some of the highest rates of Volunteers extending their service with the Peace Corps or with other aid organizations. Most Volunteers aren't mentally or physically prepared for the stresses of living independently in a developing country and navigating a foreign culture. This is not a criticism. The only way to be prepared is to do it. Some Volunteers slide seamlessly into the flow of life in their communities. Some resign after a few days, weeks, or months—from specific events back home or in their communities, but usually from the slow-burning attrition of everyday life.

I was winded by my time in Ethiopia. Not winded in the way a runner may be winded after an endurance run. I mean winded as getting the air shoved out of your lungs by an unexpected, forceful collision. I felt like that comically stupid, bad guy in a western/medieval/pirate movie who is chasing the film's hero or heroine on horseback and rides chest-first into a tree branch. Lying on my back staring up at the offending branch, I can't help thinking, should I get on my horse and keep on the chase, or should I just trot off in the other direction? Why was I chasing that guy to begin with? What would other people say if I just turned around and quit the chase? What would I think of myself?

When I told people about how exhausted I was from working in Ethiopia, I repeatedly got the "pick yourself up and get back on your horse" response. That was the polite response, and was often correct. But it didn't allow the silence needed to ask the questions that should be asked. It assumed that I should have been chasing my goal through low-hanging branches to begin with. It assumed the exhaustion and bruised self-esteem were worth the risk of helping a handful of people who fundamentally had no interest in working with foreigners who told them what they *really* needed. Is it cynical to view international aid organizations as a self-serving way to repatriate resources taken during centuries of colonial or economic rule? Are nonprofits responsible for cleaning up after foreign governments and corporations leverage cheap labor and lax laws to maximize profit? Are the children I wanted to help by building school desks the beneficiaries of my work, or are the corrupt employees that withheld local funding for those same desks? Is the small farm I created with my friend Misgano feeding the same gaunt faces of the HIV orphans used to guilt privileged donors? Too often, traditional practices careen into the guardrails placed by foreign benefactors when the cultures they comprise are forcibly pushed into the high-speed traffic of globalization by those same benefactors. These are oversimplifications. However, as the day I left Ethiopia gets farther away and I think back about my experiences there, I can say with absolute certainty, that was pretty ugly.

I am not alone in this experience. The bittersweetness of international development work is what calls many to give up the luxuries of indoor plumbing and air fryers to serve others they never met. The complexities of living and working abroad leads to dramatically different individual results depending on personality, type of work, and ability to successfully poop in a hole in the ground. Working as a couple in these conditions adds even more complexity. These experiences can strengthen or destroy relationships and may fundamentally change a person. The mental and physical abrasiveness of these experiences often leaves one feeling raw. This can provide fresh perspectives and the space to rebuild personal identities, but it can also leave people vulnerable to the fatigue that comes from contact with the world's roughest edges.

One of the most significant examples of the pretty ugly in international work is the career of photographer Kevin Carter. Carter was a member of the Bang-Bang Club, a quartet of conflict photographers that gained notoriety documenting the violence in South Africa during the transition away from the racial segregation of apartheid. Their award-winning photos of war zones gained them accolades and enemies. One of Carter's colleagues went on to teach photojournalism in the USA. Another member stepped on a land mine and lost both legs while on assignment with soldiers in Afghanistan. He was only able to return to photography after more than 80 surgeries and months of rehab. These were the most fortunate members.

Carter is best remembered for his photograph *The Vulture and the Little Girl*, documenting a stooped vulture eyeing a starving Sudanese child. Initially thought to be a girl, the child's father later revealed that the child was his son—who was able to reach aid after the picture was taken. This staggering image was published in *The New York Times* on March 26, 1993. It is as brutal as it is beautiful. The sunbaked ground is barren and light beige, which contrasts with the darkness of the vulture's feathers and the child's skin. The balance of the child and its overseer is expertly composed in the photo's frame, and perspective makes it unclear if the vulture or child is larger. It tells an emotional story. Carter won a Pulitzer Prize for the photograph the following year. The picture had pulled back the curtain hiding the human costs of the conflict in Sudan and launched Carter to fame.

That fame divided viewers of the very photograph that made him famous. Some criticized him for not helping the child in the photo, and others accused him of staging the scene. Then, in April 1994, Carter's close friend and member of the Bang-Bang Club, Ken Oosterbroek, was shot and killed by friendly fire while filming a firefight in South Africa. The cumulative traumas of

Carter's photographic accomplishments were not compatible with everyday life. His expenses were paid for by images of pain, death, and mankind's inhumanity to one another. However, even the money earned from his astounding and horrific images of famine and war was not enough to cover his debts. What is the cost of paying one's phone bill with photographs of children's corpses, when the dullness of a typical day is made possible by documenting the suffering of others? What debt is worth that?

These were questions Carter couldn't answer. On July 24, 1994, only months after winning the prestigious Pulitzer Prize, he drove his red pickup to a river near his hometown of Johannesburg, South Africa. He then fed a garden hose from the tailpipe into the cab of the truck and died from carbon monoxide poisoning. He left a brief suicide note explaining, "The pain of life overrides the joy to the point that joy does not exist." But Carter had already written a suicide note in the image of the collapsed Sudanese boy that had been printed worldwide. American essayist Susan Sontag addressed the controversy in her last published work, *Regarding the Pain of Others*,

> "There is shame as well as shock in looking at the close-up of a real horror. Perhaps the only people with the right to look at images of suffering of this extreme order are those who could do something to alleviate it…or those who could learn from it. The rest of us are voyeurs, whether or not we mean to be."

The awfully good comes at a cost.

CATHARSIS

"Live in each season as it passes; breathe the air, drink the drink, taste the fruit, and resign yourself to the influences of each."
—Henry David Thoreau

"Catharsis is about cleansing and healing at one and the same time—healing memories and attitudes, healing the spirit and the heart."
—Desmond Tutu

The grass was cool and wet from the day's rains, and the fire cast a ring of rising fog around itself as the dew fled. I laid down on the grass about ten feet from the fire, propping myself up on an elbow. Pulling sheets of paper from a stack beside me, I crumpled each piece and tossed them one by one into the fire. The flaming pile of paper, cardboard, and spent candle stubs cast a noiseless, shadowless light over the entire compound. There were no snaps or pops of smoldering twigs like a campfire would have. The flames were completely silent. Cinni, the last puppy of Titi's last litter was curled in a tight ball next to me. His mother was in California with one of our gelada monkey researcher friends, his sister was in Michigan with another researcher friend, and his brother was in Colorado with my mother. All his other siblings, past and present, were dead. He lazily raised an eyelid every time I moved to throw something into the fire. He did not know that this fire meant he would be left behind to live as a street dog, reliant on the kindness or indifference of Ethiopians or

Tikuru (left) and Cinni (right) at Negash's café shortly before Derek and Claire left Debark to return to the USA.

foreign trekkers to survive. People in town knew him, and he had a reputation of a well-behaved ferenj dog. He had a chance.

    The papers were torn from more than a dozen Peace Corps manuals, reports, and information packets that we accumulated over our two years as PCVs. It was our last night in Debark, and we had been cleaning our house all day to get ready for our departure in the morning. I was burning all our non-plastic trash to prepare for the new Volunteer who was going to move into the house next. Due to the difficulties that the Volunteer before us had had, and the challenges Claire and I had faced, this new Volunteer could be the last Volunteer Debark would have. That didn't bother me. I was just happy that we had done as much as we could. As I laid there thinking back on the past two years, I only regretted that I came to Ethiopia with such unrealistic expectations; with such delusions of optimism. I was throwing paper into the fire too slowly, and it was beginning to die down, so I walked over and dumped a stack of forms into the compost pit, now impromptu fire ring. I watched the sheets burn, blackening and peeling back from the upper corner as if the fire were reading them.

Our neighbor Selam had apparently been watching me for several minutes through the crude fence of eucalyptus poles that separated the compounds. I heard and understood her questions in Amharic as easily as if she said them in English. I allowed myself a quiet, sardonic chuckle before answering. *And now I'm leaving*.

"What's the problem?"

"There's no problem."

"OK…what are you doing?"

"Nothing…it's just a bonfire."

She inhaled sharply in acknowledgement and cast a confused glance over her shoulder as she turned and left. I'm sure it was strange seeing a lone, white guy staring into a fire in the middle of the night. My use of *demera*—the Amharic word for a celebratory fire—for a trash fire likely did nothing to ease her confusion. My vocabulary was admittedly questionable, but I knew that word. And I meant it.

I didn't question why she assumed there was a problem. Yet there was no problem—I felt great. It was one of the best moments of my life. I burned away the scraps of the bureaucracy that we had navigated the previous two years, in a garden that I had built from scratch, with a tragically loyal dog curled next to me, on a cool night at the Roof of Africa. Claire, my wife and best friend, was packing our bags just inside. We would leave our home in Ethiopia the next day. Despite wanting to visit, we would probably never return. It was just too far, too expensive, and too difficult to come back—not only because of the logistics.

The world was far from perfect while I was lying on the grass outside my Ethiopian home. After spending more than two years here, I had been robbed, punched, kicked, cursed, bitten, and pelted with rocks. However, I had also been hugged, kissed, laughed with, and stuffed full of delicious food and honey wine on countless occasions. I had had faith because I trusted that no matter what misfortune happened to us, we would get the help we needed and our American and Ethiopian friends would rally around us. Despite our dogs being hit by canes on our way to the main road, we could walk to Negash's café where they would be given fresh bread and treated like family. Despite coming home disheartened from a fruitless meeting at the park office, I could always share a meal with friends.

That half hour spent lying on the grass enjoying the signal fire of our departure was one of the most cathartic moments of my life. It was a pregnant pause that separated what life had been and what it would be. I was not scared, disappointed, sad, or conflicted. Nor was I happy. I was content. I felt like my life had meaning. I was mindful of the moment's importance, and I felt it passing without anxiety. I didn't try to prolong it or end it prematurely. When the fire had burned out, I simply stood up, patted the dog goodnight, and walked inside.

Going home. We were told for months before we left Ethiopia that moving back to the USA after living in another culture can be more difficult than adjusting to that new culture initially. Stories of depressed and jobless RPCVs sitting on parents' couches littered our minds like empty fast-food cartons. Peace Corps staff, expats, and returned Volunteers hoped to give us realistic expectations of what life would be like when we stepped foot in the States. However, this often resulted in horror stories that ended with, "But I'm sure that won't happen to you."

The strength of this reverse culture-shock is highly individualized. It depends on the culture returning from, the length of time spent in that culture, the events that transpired in that country and in the individual's home country, the personality of the individual, and numerous other factors. For RPCVs, the effect is compounded by the realities of being unemployed and couch surfing into the sunset.

Returned Volunteers can be hesitant to speak negatively about their service with people who have not experienced Peace Corps, yet will complain for hours about how much they hated their host town when with other Volunteers. This code-switching is often intended to make Peace Corps service sound better to both the people listening and the Volunteers themselves. Also, Volunteers can more easily talk about their service with people who have gone through similar experiences. Many things can be left unsaid and more meaningful dialogues can take place when a Peace Corps elevator pitch isn't required as an introduction to any overseas story. But before we could talk about our service with people back home, we had to get home.

After sleepless flights from Addis Ababa to Rome, to Bangkok, to Tokyo, to Dallas, and finally Denver, we were home. Despite all the layovers, I would still take a day of connecting flights than a day spent in a crowded, close-windowed Ethiopian bus with livestock both inside and tied to the roof. With equal parts gratitude and grogginess, we let the Jetsonian horizontal escalators carry us through the Denver International Airport. The escalators moved just slightly faster than a disgruntled Ethiopian cow weaving through the dense traffic of Addis Ababa. We were restless after our flights, but let the moving walkway set our pace.

We arrived in Denver late in the morning on Friday December 14th, and I realized why so many returning Volunteers sink into a stupor. Two years of thoughts of home had romanticized the USA. As soon as we got off the plane, we were slapped in the face by the news of the shooting at Sandy Hook Elementary School that had taken place just hours before. Really? This is the America I am coming back to? Mass shootings, the 2012 fiscal cliff, and the looming December 21st Mayan Doomsday prediction. Reality didn't reflect the end of the tunnel that returning to America was supposed to be.

FINDING SERENITY

*"Serenity is the balance between good and bad,
life and death, horrors and pleasures."*
—Norman Davies

*"We all have life storms, and when we get the rough times
and we recover from them, we should celebrate that we got
through it. No matter how bad it may seem, there's always
something beautiful that you can find."*
—Mattie JT Stepanek

How can we balance the awful and the good of international development? The math often doesn't add up the way it should—or at least the way we want it to. However, good can be found as long as we have the eyes and patience to see it. The very real struggle to survive in rural Ethiopia is a strange environment to develop optimism. The irony of finding serenity amidst fundamental life challenges is not lost on a cynic like myself.

Misgano is the only Ethiopian in this book whose name I didn't change. He shared our compound and quickly became one of our best friends. His giant smile was never forced and never failed to improve our mood. He loved sharing his culture and made sure to include us whenever appropriate. We attended the symbolic burning of large, wooden crosses for the *Meskel* holiday together, which celebrated the finding of the "true cross" by Roman Empress Saint Helena, the mother of Emperor Constantine. Watching black people in crisp, white robes burn crosses did seem like a racial reversal of the evils the Ku Klux Klan (KKK) is

Derek and Misgano celebrating the Meskel holiday.

best known for, but the Meskel ceremony was celebratory and colorful. We splashed murky holy water on each other after the river running through Debark was blessed for the Timket holiday, celebrating Jesus' baptism. These spirited feasting holidays followed days or even weeks of fasting.

Ironically, these fasting periods were some of our favorite times to eat out on the town because every restaurant had cheap, fresh, and delicious vegetarian food. Misgano introduced us to *ful*, a delicious, thick stew of fava beans, tomatoes, onions, garlic, berbere spice, and raw salt transported on camelback from the barren salt flats of the Danakil Depression. The stew simmered in shallow metal tins over a charcoal fire; a heavy layer of palm oil projecting a bubbling rainbow on its surface.

Misgano also welcomed us into his extended circle of friends, with whom we developed our own significant friendships. One friend, a tour guide, attended the English classes we held during the rainy season. He eventually moved to Europe for a tourism job, but he messaged us to say that our English class helped him succeed. He said he wouldn't have been confident enough to try for that job. And let's not forget Misgano's friend Gebre who slept on the outhouse floor to protect our house after the glass was broken out of our door. We felt safe following Misgano's judgment of people. He attracted some of the best individuals we came to know in the Simien Mountains.

Misgano was born in the mountains and was orphaned when he was young. Following the death of his last relative, he spent several days hiking from his isolated village to Debark, alone. Our landlord, himself a wonderful person, adopted Misgano despite only being several years older. Misgano was treated like a younger brother and son—depending on the situation. He worked as a bookkeeper at the Simien Lodge inside the park and helped his brother when he opened his own ecolodge near Limalimo Pass.

Looking over the Simien Mountains escarpment near Limalimo Pass.

In 2018, a wildfire burned through the Limalimo area. Misgano lost his life fighting that fire. He left a wife and small child behind, as well as a community shocked by his passing. His death galvanized efforts to improve fire response and preparedness in the park. It was too little, too late, but Misgano's sudden passing spurred much-needed conversations. He is missed by many, but he died defending what was important to him. As columnist George Crane wrote, "Appreciative words are the most powerful force for good on earth." Misgano has my sincere appreciation for all he did and all he would have done if he were still alive.

I partnered with Misgano on a grant to establish a native tree nursery. Ultimately, our tree nursery wasn't successful and became a garlic field after only one lackluster season. Poor demand and a broken irrigation pump doomed the effort, but Misgano continued advocating for tree planting and restoring forest to the Simien Mountains. Although he was not alive to see it, Ethiopia broke the world record for most trees planted in a day by organizing the planting of over 560 million trees in July 2023. This broke their own record of over 350 million trees in 2019. Misgano's death still causes my chest to tighten, but we are so grateful for the time and experiences we, and many others, had with him. That is something to find serenity in.

Sisay was our language teacher during our ten-week training before we moved to the mountains. He was brilliant, kind, and always had insights on how people from foreign cultures could work together with Ethiopians. His patience for Americans learning Amharic was nothing short of heroic. I was selected to give a speech in Amharic to thank the families that hosted our cohort of trainees. I was selected and felt comfortable giving the speech only because of Sisay's dedication and patience.

I was told during my second year of service that Sisay drowned while boating on a lake with his family. He and many others on board could not swim, so his death was inevitable once

Sisay during training at Awash National Park.

he fell overboard. Like Misgano, he died young, but left a lasting impact on Ethiopia and the PCVs who served there. That is something to find serenity in.

Nearly all the dogs I knew during our time in Ethiopia died from disease, physical injury, or poisoning by the town administration. The only three exceptions were Titi the Mama Dog and two puppies from her last litter. All three dogs had to be examined by veterinarians in Ethiopia before they could be transported. That process alone could fill a rather unpleasant book, but we had the time, resources, and determination to make it happen. Titi and one puppy went to live with gelada monkey researchers in different states. The other dog, Gobez, is ours.

His name means "clever" in Amharic and was earned before we planned to take him home. He was the first puppy of the litter to leave the small storeroom where he was born in our compound. This handsome but malnourished ball of black fluff was shipped as cargo on a passenger flight. We did not want to risk him dying before we could take him home ourselves, so we flew him home early. Lufthansa handled the connecting flights like a fine German timepiece—even getting time outside his crate in Frankfurt to stretch his legs and pee on artificial grass. He arrived safely at my mother's house in the Colorado foothills after more than 24 hours of travel, and about 8 months before we finished our service and came home ourselves.

It was a relief to have the three dogs safe in the USA, but we still had work to do in Ethiopia. Our friends, Ethiopian, American, and Other, celebrated our decision and tenacity to send the dogs to the USA. In reality, sending the dogs cost less than 500 dollars each and was only possible with the help of numerous people literally all over the world. Understandably, not everyone in our community reacted with applause. But most people didn't understand that it was much easier to take a dog to the USA than it was to take a person. In their minds, the difficulty and cost should be the same. However, you can't squeeze a person into an animal crate, load them in a plane's cargo hold, and then just release them into the welcoming wild on foreign soil.

The confusion, and occasional anger, about sending the dogs home instead of a person served as a reminder that the dogs were safe in the USA. They were dewormed, defleaed, immunized, and well-fed. Every negative statement about them became an acknowledgement of what we had accomplished to make our service and lives more meaningful. Gobez, now an old canine expat, was the best souvenir we could have brought home with us. He remains the most impactful of our attempts at the Peace Corps' third goal: Bring the world home. I'm sure this is not what JFK had in mind when he first announced the three goals. However, this long-legged, living conversation starter is also a reminder of our home in the Ethiopian highlands we left behind. I can find serenity in that.

HOW TO FAIL SUCCESSFULLY

*"Is there a solution, then, for Africa's predicament?
It's the questions I'm most often asked. It's in our nature, I
suppose, to want to be optimists, to want to think that all
problems have solutions, that even Africa might somehow, in its
own time, be 'fixed.' But this strange place defies even the
staunchest of optimists; it drains you of hope, and believe me, I
know. I'd like to say I have some magic solution, the untested
remedy for the continent's myriad ills. But the problem in Africa
is that just about everything has already been tried."*

—Keith B. Richburg

*"The place beyond despair is not hope, exactly,
but it is a place from which you may draw nearly unlimited
will, because you are no longer afraid of losing."*

—Ezekiel Kweku

There is a certain freedom in knowing you will fail because it allows the space to do what needs to be done. No matter how hard you work, how much you accomplish, or how large an impact you leave, you will fail to resolve the issues that caused the community to request a PCV in the first place. Your work will be inadequate and incomplete. Does that mean the work shouldn't be done, that it's not worth doing? Absolutely not.

This goes beyond what some psychologists call defensive pessimism, a mental strategy to increase the chances of success by setting low expectations or by planning for the worst. Peace Corps service provides ample opportunities to be surprised about how many things can go wrong. It is nearly impossible to predict all the potential challenges that arise when trying to address wicked problems. This is especially true when working in a completely different culture and environment. Acknowledging the inevitability of failure, even despite modest progress, empowers us to do what we think is impossible. Peace Corps is not as effective as it is because it creates saviors and sends them to solve problems that no one else could solve. Peace Corps works because it brings US citizens into compassion with citizens of another country. Whether washing clothes by hand, attending a host family wedding, or shopping at the market, PCVs never stop working. They are a personal bridge between the USA and the country they serve. That is a heavy responsibility. Volunteers are the everyday ambassadors that expose their communities to an image of America beyond *Keeping up with the Kardashians*, school shootings, and its political squabbling.

As cultural ambassadors from a more powerful country, the everyday opinions and actions of Volunteers carry weight. Even minor interactions can shift perceptions in relatively isolated rural communities. One surprising example of this was who we bought eggs from at the market. Eggs were one of our staple foods in Ethiopia, they were cheap, costing only about 2 cents each, and available year-round. We went to the market two to three times a week and bought a few eggs every time. They were sold in flimsy plastic bags, so we couldn't buy many at once without risking them cracking against each other or ripping the bag. One day, as we were walking by the egg vendors, we were greeted by a flat-chested woman with a mustache. In a country where homosexuality is punishable by jail time, transexual and non-binary people are not visible in public places. They are there, but they must hide for their safety and the safety of their families. This is the reality in much of Africa.

The woman had eggs in a canvas bag at her feet, with feet turned inward to protect them. She introduced herself as Birtucaan, which literally means "orange" in Amharic. She was in the market surrounded by a dozen others also selling eggs, a job traditionally done by women. But her androgynous features made her stand out. Her smile was genuine as she showed us her eggs—too many eggs. It was obvious they were not selling well, just as obvious as all the eggs in the market were the same in quality and price. Customers bought from their dabeñña, the person they always bought from. Without established social ties, it was nearly impossible for someone new to start selling something successfully.

She was friendly and not pushy, despite a clear need to sell more eggs. So, we purchased from her and continued with our normal shopping. We purchased from her again, and again, and again. Birtucaan became our egg dabeñña. We noticed that she no longer had trouble selling her eggs, and the women

Women selling produce at stalls in Debark's main market.

around her sat closer. Birtucaan began blending into the market instead of standing apart. We had to start looking for her when we needed eggs. I asked an acquaintance why her eggs were now more popular. "Because you buy them," he responded. The power of our buying habits had opened the door for a small, but fundamental change. Volunteers don't need grandiose gestures to have an impact in their communities. Who they talk to can be more powerful than any project they devote their time to.

Ethiopia has been able to concurrently foster feelings of national pride and communal helplessness. It owes its current success—its existence—as a nation-state from being able to attract aid from others. Due to the famine in the 1980s, many international aid organizations have established their headquarters in Addis Ababa. With the construction of the new African Union (AU) compound, Addis Ababa is quickly becoming the functional capital of the entire continent. Practically none of the 200-million-dollar bill for the gargantuan AU compound came from Africa itself. The construction was a "gift" from the Chinese government which has billions of dollars invested in Ethiopian infrastructure and has been "gifted" thousands of hectares of fertile land in return. China is not alone in providing these conditional investments. Ethiopia is usually in the top five foreign aid recipients for many industrialized nations. International conflicts, such as in Ukraine and the Middle East, have shuffled the numbers, but Ethiopia is still firmly on the leaderboard.

I learned the concept of tolerance stacks from an engineer friend of mine. The concept is equally applicable to airplanes, pocket calculators, pencils, and even cultures. Many systems, whether mechanical, ecological, or social, operate within a range of tolerances. These ranges are determined by the components of the system and the connections between them. The system works fine if all the components are working within a range of conditions. If something is off a little bit here and a little bit there, the system can usually still function. Yet, when a system is full of these tiny deviations, the tolerances stack up and the system won't function as well or may stop working altogether.

It is relatively easy to say that a component of a machine is too far from a certain standard to function—too wide, too narrow, too brittle, too flexible. On the other hand, it is nearly impossible to say whether an entire culture is "running rough" and relentlessly grinding away its gears. Not just nearly impossible, it is also dangerous. Racism and xenophobia are easy to camouflage behind cultural criticisms. The concept is imperfect when applied to fluid and complex systems like social interactions, but still applicable. Development work often treats complex, nested systems like simple machines with inputs and outputs, yet fails to recognize the intolerances as they stack up.

I may be disillusioned when it comes to Africa's development, but having spoken to dozens of people who have been drained of their passion and optimism on the continent, I know I am not alone. On the other hand, there are also hundreds of incredible people doing amazing work all over the continent. Unfortunately, and misleadingly, in the never-ending quest for future funding, it is usually these success stories that get pushed to the surface of the mainstream. The lion's share of unsuccessful projects drifts to the bottom. No one likes to advertise a failure, and for NGOs, highlighting a failure could mean a decline in funding.

Unfortunately, "what should be," "what could be," and

"what is" are completely different realities. One can say the same for most countries, although in most countries, this failure to be "what could be" is not a matter of life and death. I do not mean something as prosaic as human death, but rather the death of an entire landscape; the ability of a place to support life. Of course, Ethiopia will always have something green. I am not so pessimistic and disheartened to think that there will be a time when nothing grows here. It is rather the loss of richness and potential that will never be restored without significant changes. The trend lines are enough to make an optimist cry.

Claire and I worked with a group of dedicated teachers and parents to expand and renovate an existing primary school library, and to have desks built for 600 students. The library had rarely been used by students and almost never used by teachers, because most of the books had been donated and were in the languages of the foreign tourists who donated them. The classrooms all had dirt floors and inadequate seating, which meant many of the students had to stand, sit on the floor, or cram with four others on desks built for two.

With the hard work of the teachers, grant funding, and generous donations from friends and family, we were able to make a significant impact. The school threw an over-the-top thank-you ceremony for us, and Peace Corps in general. A local government representative came to personally thank us for our work and to present us with gifts the school had bought for us. Even though he came an hour late, he gave a passionate speech on the importance of education for Ethiopia's development and promised money to the school to help renovate some of the classrooms.

Weeks before any of this happened, the federal Ethiopian government agreed on a national pay increase for teachers. Local teachers were paid between 1,200 and 1,800 birr a month

Derek and Claire celebrating the library and classroom desk project at the community ceremony.

depending on education and experience. At the time, this was between 70 and 100 dollars per month. This was nearly impossible to support a family on, even in rural Ethiopia. The local government refused to honor the pay increase shortly after our thank-you ceremony. Teachers from the school we worked with, as well as teachers from other nearby schools, went on strike to demand the higher pay they had been told they would receive. The man who shook our hands at the ceremony, who gave a homily on the importance of education, authorized the detention and physical punishment of the protesting teachers. Teachers who dedicated their personal time, energy, and even money to improve their school were rewarded by being beaten and humiliated. They were released with the knowledge that if they went on strike again, they would likely be tried as terrorists.

At the time the teachers were detained, I read a book by the religious author Max Lucado about making a difference in other people's lives. I had enjoyed reading some of his other work. In this book, he includes several examples of situations in Ethiopia where people made a difference. Most of these were part of World Vision projects. Lucado, a modern-day Saint Augustine, declares that, "Poverty is not the lack of charity, but the lack of justice." He then goes on to glorify the charity of religious organizations. There are no discussions of justice or helping people achieve it. The book is page after page of celebrating faith-based charity. Lucado talks about looking at people instead of looking through them and then ignores his own advice. People must work for their own justice—it cannot be gifted to them. One can, and should, stand with people to achieve justice. However, and pardon the cliché, one cannot carry their crosses for them. Too often in Ethiopia, well-intentioned people behave charitably and end up giving people gold-gilded nails to crucify themselves with. It may be prettier, but it is still a broken person bleeding out on a broken tree.

Charity counts for nothing until justice is served. Lucado tells a heartfelt story about a man who needed an ox to plow his field to support his family. What Lucado doesn't mention, and may not even know, is that the farmer doesn't own the land he is working and must pay the Ethiopian government to even be allowed on it. All land in Ethiopia was nationalized after the emperor was overthrown. The farmer may have been permitted to farm the land after it was taken away from someone else. Lucado doesn't mention that the shallow depth of Ethiopian plows creates a compacted layer of clay, called a hardpan, just below the soil surface. The hardpan not only reduces crop yield but also increases the likelihood of erosion because roots cannot penetrate the hardpan and the soil above sloughs off in heavy rain. Lucado sees a poor man without an ox. Give the man an ox. Problem solved. Justice served. Poverty averted. If only.

For international development organizations to accomplish any work at all, they force themselves to be optimistic. They convince themselves that problems are simple, unambiguous, and can be solved with enough funding. Regrettably, their own survival as institutions is at stake because they must present a productive, happy face to their donors to keep funds flowing. By necessity, the first goal of many organizations is not to bring about some positive change in the world, but to persuade donors that they already are bringing change.

While traveling abroad shortly before joining the Peace Corps, I spotted a thrift store advertising fair trade goods from women's cooperatives in Africa. I noticed a quote painted on the back wall as I perused the woven baskets, soda can sculptures, and primitivist wood carvings. It struck me as so important that I took a picture of the mural and walked out of the store feeling a better person for having read it. The quote was, "It is better to light a candle than to curse the darkness. —Chinese proverb."

What could be praised as a piece of ancient wisdom, I now place alongside such tired sayings as, "Today is the first day of the rest of your life." What may be sufficient guidance for college existentialists, offers very little in the way of helping someone to actually "carpe diem."

Which revered monk gifted the world the wisdom I read on the shop wall? It has been attributed to Confucius. Although, it has also been attributed to JFK, Eleanor Roosevelt, and other credibility boosters. The truth is that it came from a sermon by an obscure, lanky Methodist minister in England named W.L. Watkinson. Would I have been as drawn to the words if I knew who wrote them? Maybe, but probably not.

"It is better to light a candle than to curse the darkness." Yes, but you still need to curse the darkness from time to time, so you don't forget why you lit the candle in the first place. This may seem silly. How can you forget to bring light into the darkness? Unfortunately, it happens more often than you might think—especially in international development. The result is a room full of candles and people wondering what a candle is and how one lights it. I'm obviously taking liberties with the metaphor, but there are real-world consequences from this mindset. Someone will hear about this group of people sitting in the dark and may send them even more candles or train them on the proper way to light a candle. That may be enough, but international interventions are rarely that clearcut. The end result is often the same...same room, same darkness, same people.

The world is full of people who have made industries out of cursing the darkness. Combative media outlets, televangelists, and US Congress come to mind. Hand them a candle, however, and they probably won't know what to do with it. Someone might even start an awareness campaign about how candles are infringing the right of darkness to exist, or how candles steal oxygen. There clearly must be a balance between cursing and lighting, but if you want to help someone brighten their own dark room, you need to make sure they can curse before you give them a light.

Africans are better recognized as problem tolerators than problem solvers. That does not mean that there aren't people who are passionate and innovative. Keeping the peace and avoiding shame—at least within the same ethnic group—are far more important than working to improve the situation. The problem might be solved later, but it won't be worth it if those relationships break down in the process. This is where the pictures of smiling African children come from—my life may be dark, but it is better to avoid the problem than to let it consume my thoughts. I'm not making a value judgment on this mentality because Western countries would do well to learn a little from this approach. Every culture has the right to self-determination, i.e., the right to choose where it wants to go and how it gets there. Along with that right, however, are the consequences of those choices.

I was determined to light as many candles as I could once my feet hit African soil. I wanted to come back to the USA with a calloused thumb and a trail of empty lighters behind me. Scenes of famine, disease, and deforestation boiled in my mind as I tried to find some cause worth living for. Dying for a cause can be very easy, especially when a person doesn't care about how others will be impacted. Living for a cause is infinitely more difficult. I realized that many of the things I had set out to do were already the responsibilities of people who were choosing not to do them or were airdropping candles. Ethiopia had the last ruling emperor in the world. The Solomonic Dynasty ended when Haile Selassie was assassinated following a military coup in the early 1970s. The Conquering Lion of the Tribe of Judah, His Imperial Majesty Haile Selassie I, King of Kings, Lord of Lords, Elect of God, Ras Tefari, was 82 years old when he was strangled to death in his bed. If he failed so gloriously, what chance did mortals like us have?

Africa needs more deep-pocket development projects and missionaries about as much as it needs spray tans and low-carb meal replacement bars. Africa does not *need* Peace Corps Volunteers or any other type of development volunteers for that matter. That is not meant to discourage but rather to inspire in the right direction. Foreigners cannot be saviors, but they can be friends, coworkers, change-makers, and people willing to serve. Don't be afraid to pick up a fiddle and try to scratch out a pleasant, simple tune.

EPILOGUE

"The only man I envy is the man who has not yet been to Africa—for he has so much to look forward to."

—Richard Mullins

My current life is far removed from Ethiopia. I have a full-time faculty job at the university where I spent many years as a student. I have a daughter. I have gained weight and lost hair. I have a mortgage. The two bedrooms and two (two!) indoor bathrooms seem cavernous compared to the 200 square feet of mud and eucalyptus poles that I shared with my wife and a cadre of dogs a lifetime ago.

When asked if I would serve as a PCV again, I answer the question before it is even finished. YES. My years in the Peace Corps were the worst and best two years of my life. There wasn't a week that went by that I didn't contemplate leaving Ethiopia. Yet, every week I found reasons to stay. The mental math always came out in favor of trying to make it work, trying to do better by our community and ourselves. Before I joined the Peace Corps, I heard nothing but good things about Ethiopia. I heard the hospitality was unrivaled, the scenery was incredible, and that the people could withstand any hardship with a smile. These were all true—at times. As Volunteers, we were told not to come with expectations, which is good advice—at times. I expected Ethiopia to be challenging, but all the positive things I had heard couldn't prepare me for the reality of living there.

If there is a message in this mess of belligerent tangents, it is this: Believe all the good things you have heard about the Peace Corps. No, really. They are genuinely true, even if they do not seem true at first. Peace Corps is an incredible, matchless experience. It has a tremendous impact on the people who embrace the uncertainty and get on the plane to a country they have likely never been to, and possibly never heard of.

BUT along with the good, PCVs can expect to be challenged in ways they never imagined. They can expect to be uncomfortable in ways they never thought possible. Expect to doubt the validity of their desire to stay. Expect to doubt their ability to co-create positive change in their community. Expect to cry from the things they will see and experience. Expect to miss friends and family more than they thought possible. Expect to miss things they never thought they would miss—like predictable bowel movements, a favorite breakfast cereal, and not having fleas.

However, they must remember that if someone is mean, it is not because they are from that certain country, it is because they are an ass, had a bad day, are mentally ill, or several of the above. If someone steals from them, it is not because they are from that country, it is because they are a thief. And if someone laughs at them when they speak, it is not because they are from that country, but because they are not used to foreigners trying to speak their native language.

PCVs fail. They fail big, and they fail often. Embracing those failures is a large part of what it means to be a PCV. Writing this book was one of the hardest things I have done, not because I dislike writing or because of the time committed to finishing it. Writing this book made me relive all the wondrous failures I had as a Peace Corps Volunteer. Thank you for sharing that with me.

REFERENCES

Abera, K., & Kinahan, A. A. (2011). Factors Affecting Fire Extent and Frequency in the Bale Mountains National Park. *Journal of the Ethiopian Wildlife and Natural History Society*, Special Ed, 146–157.

Admassie, Y. (2000). *Twenty Years to Nowhere: Property Rights, Land Management and Conservation in Ethiopia*. The Red Sea Press, Inc.

Alemayehu, M. (2012). Ethiopia: An Early Warning for a Famine in 2013. *Ethiopian Review*.

Alemayehu, K. (2012). Population viability analysis of Walia ibex (*Capra walie*) at Simien Mountains National Park (SMNP), Ethiopia. *African Journal of Ecology*, 1, 1–8.

Alemayehu, K., Dessie, T., Gizaw, S., Haile, A., & Mekasha, Y. (2011). Population dynamics of Walia ibex (*Capra walie*) at Simien Mountains National Park, Ethiopia. *African Journal of Ecology*, 49, 292–300.

Amhara National Regional State. (2007). 2007 Population and Housing Census of Ethiopia: Statistical Report for Amhara Region.

Amhara National Regional State, & Simen Mountains National Park Integrated Development Project. (2004). *SMNP-IDP*.

Andualem Imiru, G. (2012). An Identification of Critical Strategic Success Factors that Makes Ethiopia One of the Most Attractive Tourist Destination. *International Journal of Research in Commerce IT & Management*, 2(5), 25–31.

Ashley, C., & Mitchell, J. (2007). Assessing how tourism revenues reach the poor.

Awokuse, T. O. (2011). FOOD AID IMPACTS ON RECIPIENT DEVELOPING COUNTRIES : A REVIEW OF EMPIRICAL METHODS AND EVIDENCE. *Journal of International Development*, 23, 493–514.

Axelrod, R. (2001). Crafting Effective Policy in a Contentious and Complex World. In S. E. Daniels & G. B. Walker (Eds.), *Working Through Environmental Conflict: The Collaborative Learning Approach* (pp. 1–13). Praeger.

Azarnert, L. (2008). Foreign Aid, Fertility and Human Capital Accumulation. *Economica*, 75, 766–781.

Balint, P. J., Stewart, R. E., Desai, A., & Walters, L. C. (2006). Managing Wicked Environmental Problems: Integrating Public Participation and Adaptive Management.

Ball, R., & Johnson, C. (1996). Political, economic and humanitarian motivations for PL 480 Food Aid: evidence from Africa. *Economic Development and Cultural Change*, 44, 515–547.

Barnes, T. A., J. F. Dwyer, E. K. Mojica, P. A. Petersen, and R. E. Harness. (2022). Wildland fires ignited by avian electrocutions. *Wildlife Society Bulletin*. 46(3), E1302.

BBC, & Discovery Channel. (2011, February 10). Mountains (Season 1, Episode 5). *Human Planet*. Discovery Channel.

Beegle, K., Christiaensen, L. (2019). Accelerating Poverty Reduction in Africa. Washington, DC: World Bank

Beehner, J. C., Gebre, B., Bergman, T., & McCann, C. (2008). POPULATION ESTIMATE FOR GELADAS (THEROPITHECUS GELADA) LIVING IN AND AROUND THE SIMIEN MOUNTAINS NATIONAL PARK, ETHIOPIA. Unpublished proof.

Behnke, R., & Metaferia, F. (2011). The Contribution of Livestock to the Ethiopian Economy – Part II.

Bekele-Tesemma, A. (2007). *Useful Trees and Shrubs for Ethiopia: Identification, Propagation and Management for 17 Agroclimatic Zones*.

Bergman, T. (2011). Recommendations for the Management of the Simien Mountains National Park.

Berkes, F., & Berkes, M. K. (2009). Ecological complexity, fuzzy logic, and holism in indigenous knowledge. *Futures*, 49, 6–12.

Borg, Marcus. (2014). *Speaking Christian*. Harper One.

Bongers, F., & Tennigkeit, T. (2010). Degraded Forests in Eastern Africa: Introduction. In F. Bongers & T. Tennigkeit (Eds.), *Degraded Forests in Eastern Africa: Management and Restoration* (pp. 1–18). Earthscan.

Brown, V., Deane, P., Harris, J., & Russell, J. (2010). Towards a Just and Sustainable Future. Tackling Wicked Problems (pp. 3–15).

Central Statistical Agency. (2005). The Impact of Education on Health Outcomes: A new look at data from the 2005 Ethiopia demographic and Health Survey.

Chala, D., Brochmann, C., Psomas, A., Ehrich, D., Gizaw, A., Masao, C. A., Bakkestuen, V., & Zimmermann, N. E. (2016). Good-bye to tropical alpine plant giants under warmer climates? Loss of range and genetic diversity in Lobelia rhynchopetalum. *Ecology and evolution*, 6(24), 8931–8941.

Charnely, S., & Poe, M. R. (2007). Community Forestry in Theory and Practice: Where Are We Now? *Annual Review of Anthropology*, 36, 301–336.

Chief Reporter. (2011, February 20). Ministers axe foreign aid to half the current countries. *The Sunday Telegraph*.

Colfer, C.J.P. (Ed.). (2005). *The Equitable Forest: Diversity, Community, and Resource Management*. Resources for the Future Press.

Colfer, Carol J. Pierce, & Byron, Y. (2001). Security of Intergenerational Access to Resources. In Carol J. Pierce Colfer & Y. Byron (Eds.), *People Managing Forests*. Resources for the Future Press.

Cornwall, A., & Jewkes, R. (1995). What is Participatory Research? *Social Science Methods*, 41, 1667–1676.

Council of Ministers Wildlife Development, Conservation and Utilization Council of Ministers Regulations No. 163/2008 (2008).

Dabelko, G. D. (2006). USAID Environmental Change and Security Program Report.

Debonnet, G., Melamari, L., & Bomhard, B. (2006). Reactive Monitoring Mission to Simien Mountains National Park (pp. 1–26).

Denny, C. (2002). Third world seeks justice through fair trade. *Guardian Weekly*, pp. 10–16.

Dercon, S., & Hoddinott, J. (2005). Livelihoods, Growth, and Links to Market Towns in 15 Ethiopian Villages.

Dessie, G., & Erkossa, T. (2011). Eucalyptus in East Africa: Socio-economic and environmental issue.

Devereux, S. (2000). Food Security in Ethiopia: A Discussion Paper for Department of International Development.

Falch, F. (2000). *Simien Mountains National Park Management Plan*.

Farsani, N. T., Coelho, C., & Costa, C. (2011). Geotourism and Geoparks as Novel Strategies for Socio-economic Development in Rural Areas. *International Journal of Tourism Research*, 13, 68–81.

Federal Democratic Republic of Ethiopia. (1997). Agricultural Wage Employment and Rural Non-farm Employment in Ethiopia.

Fentene, M., Gashaw, M., Nauke, P., & Beck, E. (1998). Microclimate and ecophysiological significance of the tree-like life-form of *Lobelia rhynochopetalum* in an alpine environment. *Oecologia*, 113, 332–340.

Fishpool, L., & Evans, M. (Eds.). (2001). *Important Bird Areas in Africa and Associated Islands: Priority Sites for Conservation*. Pisces Publications and BirdLife International.

Ford Foundation. (1998). Forestry for Sustainable Rural Development.

Forum for Social Studies, & University of Sussex. (2001). Natural Resource Management in Ethiopia. In A. Pankhurst (Ed.), *Natural Resource Management in Ethiopia*.

Frahm, J.-P. (1990). Bryophyte Phytomass in Tropical Ecosystems. *Botanical Journal of the Linnean Society*, 104, 23–33.

Frankfurt Zoological Society. (2008). *Simien Mountains National Park General Management Plan* 2009-2019.

Garrett, J. (2005). Dynamic Livelihoods: Making the Most of Rural-Urban Connections (No. 194) (pp. 1–2).

Gelan, A. U. (2007). Does Food Aid Have Disincentive Effects on Local Production? A General Equilibrium Perspective on Food Aid in Ethiopia. *Food Policy,* 32, 436–458.

Gerber, P., Steinfeld, H., Wassenaar, T., Castel, V., Rosales, M., & De Haan, C. (2006). Livestock's Long Shadow: Environmental Issues and Options (pp. 1–408). UN Food and Agriculture Organization.

Gilligan, D. O., & Hoddinott, J. (2006). Is There Persistence in the Impact of Emergency Food Aid? Evidence on Consumption, Food Security, and Assets in Rural Ethiopia.

Girma A, Aemiro A. (2022). Prevalence and Associated Risk Factors of Intestinal Parasites and Enteric Bacterial Infections among Selected Region Food Handlers of Ethiopia during 2014-2022: A Systematic Review and Meta-Analysis. *Scientific World Journal.* 2022: 7786036

Global Humanitarian Assistance. (2010). Humanitarian financing to Ethiopia 2000-2010.

Gordon, F. L., & Carillet, J.-B. (2003). *Ethiopia & Eritrea* (2nd Edition). Oakland: Lonely Planet Publications.

Grunenfelder, J. (2005). Livestock in the Simen Mountains, Ethiopia. University of Berne.

Guinand, Y. (2001). Towards integrated food security through subsidised employment and income generation activities (pp. 1–17).

Guinand, Y., & Ugas, M. (1999). Underdeveloped, drought prone, food insecure: reflections on living conditions in parts of the Simien Mountains.

HaileMeskal, F., Kitaw, Y., & Dejene, A. (2008). Follow up National Survey On the Harmful Traditional Practices in Ethiopia.

Hall, D., & Richards, G. (2000). *Tourism and Sustainable Community Development.* Routledge.

Harrower MJ, Dumitru IA, Perlingieri C, et al. (2019). Beta Samati: discovery and excavation of an Aksumite town. *Antiquity.* 93(372),1534-1552.

Hedburg, O. (1951). Vegetation belts of the east African mountains. Svensk Botanisk Tidskrift, 451, 140–204.

Hochschwender, J., Gebrewold, F., & Abuhay, S. (2000). ETHIOPIA MICROENTERPRISE SECTOR ASSESSMENT: A Summary Report to Assist Implementation of the USAID/Ethiopia Strategy SO3 (pp. 1–82).

Human Rights Watch. (2010). Development without Freedom: How Aid Underwrites Repression in Ethiopia.

Hurni, H. (1986). *Management Plan: Simen Mountains National Park and Surrounding Rural Area.*

Hurni, H., & Ludi, E. (2000). Reconciling Conservation with Sustainable Development.

Institute of Biodiversity Conservation. (2005). *National Biodiversity Strategy and Action Plan.*

Jackson, W. J., & Ingles, A. W. (1998). *Participatory Techniques for Community Forestry: A Field Manual.* IUNC and The Worldwide Fund For Nature.

Johnson, N., Mansfield, K. L., Marston, D. A., Goddard, T., Wilson, C., Fooks, A. R., & Selden, D. (2010). A new outbreak of rabies in rare Ethiopian wolves (Canis simensis). *Archives of Virology*, 155, 1175–1177.

Kirwan, B., & McMillan, M. (2007). Food Aid and Poverty. *American Journal of Agricultural Economics*, 89(5), 1152–1160.

Kirwan, L. P. (1972). The Christian Topography and the Kingdom of Axum. *The Geographical Journal*, 138(2), 166–177.

Klooster, D., & Masera, O. (2000). Community forest management in Mexico: carbon mitigation and biodiversity conservation through rural development. *Global Environmental Change*, 10, 259–272.

Kuris, Ayele. (2006). *The Ethiopian Economy* (Second Edi.).

Lefevre, B., & Pinard, M. (2011). Traditional Beekeeping and Patterns of Host Tree Use in the Harenna Forest, Bale Mountains National Park. *Journal of the Ethiopian Wildlife and Natural History Society*, Special Ed, 208–212.

Levinsohn, J., & Mcmillan, M. (2007). Does Food Aid Harm the Poor? Household Evidence from Ethiopia. In A. Harrison (Ed.), *Globalization and Poverty* (pp. 561–596). University of Chicago Press.

Macro International Inc. (2007). Trends in Demographic and Reproductive Health Indicators in Ethiopia. Macro International Inc.

Makhado, Z., & Kepe, T. (2006). Crafting a Livelihood: Local Level Trade in Mats and Baskets in Pondoland, South Africa. *Development Southern Africa*, 23, 497–509.

Marcus, H. G. (2002). *A History of Ethiopia.* University of California Press.

Marino, J. (2003). Threatened Ethiopian wolves persist in small isolated Afroalpine enclaves. *Oryx*, 37, 62–71.

Martin, D. (2008, August). Ecotourism in Ethiopia. Le Monde Diplomatique.

Matthews, C. (2006). Livestock a major threat to environment: Remedies urgently needed. FAO Newsroom.

Mendick, Robert. (2011). Ministers axe foreign aid to half the current countries. *The Sunday Telegraph*. 20 February 2011.

Mengistu, A. A., Loader, S., Getahun, A., Saber, S., & Nagel, P. (2011). Conservation of Ethiopian Amphibians: A Race Against Time. *Journal of the Ethiopian Wildlife and Natural History Society*, Special Ed, 93–93.

Mitchell, J., Coles, C., Abate, F. M., Egziabihar, M., Posthumus, H., Johannes, A., Uliwa, P., et al. (2009). Enhancing private sector and community engagement in tourism services in Ethiopia. 44, 1–104. Overseas Development Institute.

Moore, J., Balmford, A., Allnut, T., & Burgess, N. D. (2004). Integrating costs into conservation planning across Africa. *Biological Conservation*, 117, 343–350.

Myers, N. (1996). The World's Forests: Problems and Potentials. *Environmental Conservation*, 23(2), 156–168.

Nageli, R. (1978). Debark (Simen) - A Market Town in the Highland of Ethiopia. *Geographica Bernensia*, 1, 73–91.

Narayanasamy, N. (2009). *Participatory Rural Appraisal: Principles, Methods and Application*. Sage Publications India.

National Research Council. (1999). Our Common Journey. National Academy Press.

Nägeli, R., & Zurbuchen, M. (1978). Debark: functional structure of an Ethiopian market town.

Negash, L. (2010). *A selection of Ethiopia's Indigenous Trees: Biology, Uses and Propagation Techniques*. Addis Ababa University Press.

Nemomissa, S., & Puff, C. (2001). Flora and Vegetation of the Simen Mountains National Park, Ethiopia. *Biologiske Skrifter*, 54, 335–348.

Nicol, C. W. (1971). *From the Roof of Africa*. Alfred A. Knopf, Inc.

OBf. (2009). Assessment of the Value of the Protected Area System of Ethiopia, *Making the Economic Case*. (Vol. II, pp. 1–100).

Oltheten, T. M. P. (1995). Participatory Approaches to Planning for Community Forestry. Rome.

Pankhurst, R. (1990). *A Social History of Ethiopia. The Northern and Central Highlands from Early Medieval Times to the Rise of Emperor Tewõdros II*. Institute of Ethiopian Studies, Addis Ababa University.

Pankhurst, R. (2006). Historical notes on books: An early Ethiopian map. Richard Pankhurst Historical and cultural articles on Ethiopia. Retrieved March 12, 2013, http://richardpankhurst.wordpress.com/2008/05/06/historical-notes-on-books-an-early-ethiopian-map/

Peace Corps. (2012). Mission.

Pellizzoni, L. (2003). Uncertainty and participatory democracy. *Environmental Values*, 12, 195–224.

Pereira, T., Shackleton, C., & Shackleton, S. (2006). Trade in Reed-Based Craft Products in Rural Villages in the Eastern Cape, South Africa. *Development Southern Africa*, 23, 477–95.

Pocs, T. (1976). The role of epiphytic vegetation in the water balance and humus production of the rain forests of the Uluguru Mountains, East Africa. *Boissiera*, 24, 499–503.

Puff, C., & Nemomissa, S. (2005). PLANTS OF THE SIMEN (Vol. 37). National Botanic Garden of Belgium.

Rahman, M. T., Sobur, M. A., Islam, M. S., Ievy, S., Hossain, M. J., El Zowalaty, M. E., Rahman, A. T., & Ashour, H. M. (2020). Zoonotic Diseases: Etiology, Impact, and Control. *Microorganisms*, 8(9), 1405.

Rami, H. (2002). Food aid is not development: A system that intends to improve food security when done poorly, achieves the opposite.

RESAL Ethiopia. (2000). Income Diversification in Amhara: The Need for a Strategy.

Riba, M. (1998). Effects of intensity and frequency of crown damage on resprouting of Erica arborea L. (Ericaceae). *Acta Oecologica*, 19(1), 9–16.

Richburg, Keith. (2009). *Out of America: A Black Man Confronts Africa*. Basic Books.

Ridgewell, A., & Flintan, F. (2007). Livelihoods & Income Development in Ethiopia. In *Gender & Pastoralism Volume II* (pp. 1–105).

Rittel, H. W. J., & Webber, M. M. (1973). Dilemmas in a General Theory of Planning. *Policy Sciences*, 4(2), 155–169.

Sahlins, M., & Service, E. R. (2001). Adaptation, Culture Scale, and the Environmental Crisis. In J. H. Bodley (Ed.), *Anthropology and Contemporary Human Problems* (4th ed., pp. 23–64). Mayfield Publishing Company.

Salafsky, N., Cauley, H., Balachander, G., Cordes, B., Parks, J., Margoluis, C., Bhatt, S., et al. (2001). Systematic Test of an Enterprise Strategy for Community-Based Biodiversity Conservation. *Conservation Biology*, 15, 1585–1595.

Shields, M. (2013). Gunmen kill Austrian rafter in Ethiopia. Reuters. Retrieved January 10, 2013, http://www.reuters.com/article/2013/01/07/uk-austria-ethiopia-idUSLNE90602M20130107

Shiferaw, F., & Laurenson, K. (2011). Risk of Disease Transmission Between Domestic Livestock and Wild Ungulates in the Bale Mountains National Park, Ethiopia. *Journal of the Ethiopian Wildlife and Natural History Society*, Special Ed, 269–281.

Shrader-Frechette, K. S., & McCoy, E. D. (1993). Method in Ecology: Strategies for Conservation. Cambridge University Press.

Sillero-Zubiri, C., & Gottelli, D. (1995). Spatial organization in the Ethiopian wolf *Canis simensis:* Large packs and small stable home ranges. *Journal of Zoology London*, 237, 65–81.

Sillero-zubiri, C., Gottelli, D., Marino, J., Randall, D., Tallents, L., & Macdonald, D. W. (2011). Ecology and Reproductive Strategy of an Afroalpine Specialist: Ethiopian Wolves in the Bale Mountains. *Journal of the Ethiopian Wildlife and Natural History Society*, Special Ed, 61–79.

Sillero-Zubiri, C. & Marino, J. (2004). *Canis simiensis*. In *IUCN 2004*. 2004 IUCN Red List of Threatened Species.

Small, S. A. (1995). Action-Oriented Research: Models and Methods. *Journal of Marriage and Family*, 57, 941–955.

Spevacek, A. (2011). USAID and Predecessor Loans and Grants / Food Aid to Ethiopia.

Stattersfield, A., & et al. (1998). Endemic Bird Areas of the world: Priorities for their conservation. Birdlife International.

Sterck, F. J., Couralet, C., Nangendo, G., Wassie, A., Sahle, Y., Sass-Klaassen, U., Markesteijn, L., et al. (2010). Juniperus procera (Cupressaceae) in Afromontane Forests in Ethiopia: From Tree Growth and Population Dynamics to Sustainable Forest Use. In F. Bongers & T. Tennigkeit (Eds.), *Degraded Forests in Eastern Africa: Management and Restoration* (pp. 291–304). Earthscan.

Suhail, M., & Thirubhuvan, J. (2009). Sustainable Tourism Mechanism for the Development of Tourism in Ethiopia - A Key Factor to Sustain Economy.

Suich, H., & Murphy, C. (2002). Crafty women: The livelihood impact of craft income in Caprivi.

Tadesse, D., Williams, S., & Irwin, B. (2011). People in National Parks - Joint Natural Resource Management in Bale Mounatians National Park - Why it Makes Sense to Work with Local People. *Journal of the Ethiopian Wildlife and Natural History Society*, Special Ed, 257–268.

Tadesse, G., & Shively, G. (2009). Food Aid, Food Prices, And Producer Disincentives in Ethiopia. *American Journal of Agricultural Economics*, 91(4), 942–955.

Tainter, J. A. (2001). Sustainable Rural Communities. In Carol J. Pierce Colfer & Y. Byron (Eds.), *People Managing Forests*. Resources for the Future Press.

Teketay, D., Lemenih, M., Bekele, T., Yemshaw, Y., Feleke, S., Tadesse, W., Moges, Y., et al. (2010). Forest Resources and Challenges of Sustainable Forest Management and Conservation in Ethiopia. In F. Bongers & T. Tennigkeit (Eds.), *Degraded Forests in Eastern Africa: Management and Restoration* (pp. 19–64). Earthscan.

Tessema, M. E., Lilieholm, R. J., Ashenafi, Z., & Leader-Williams, N. (2010). Community Attitudes Toward Wildlife and Protected Areas in Ethiopia. *Society and Natural Resources*, 23, 489–506.
UNESCO World Heritage Committee. (2006). DECISIONS ADOPTED AT THE 30TH SESSION OF THE WORLD HERITAGE COMMITTEE.
United Nations. (2008). The Millennium Development Goals Report 2008.
United Nations. (2012). The Millennium Development Goals Report 2012.
United Nations, Department of Economic and Social Affairs, Population Division. (2015). World Population Prospects: The 2015 Revision, Key Findings and Advance Tables. Working Paper No. ESA/P/WP.241.
United Nations Environment Programme. (2011). SIMIEN NATIONAL PARK ETHIOPIA (Vol. 29).
Vial, F., Macdonald, D. W., & Haydon, D. T. (2011). Livestock Grazing in the Bale Mountains National Park, Ethiopia: Past, Present and Future. *Journal of the Ethiopian Wildlife and Natural History Society*, Special Ed, 197–207.
Vial, F., Sillero-zubiri, C., Marino, J., Haydon, D. T., & Macdonald, D. W. (2010). An analysis of long-term trends in the abundance of domestic livestock and free-roaming dogs in the Bale Mountains National Park, Ethiopia. *African Journal of Agricultural Research*, 49, 91–102.
Walpole, M. (2004). Community scouts promote conservation and livelihood security in the Mara ecosystem, Kenya. *Sustainable Development International*, 10, 119–121.
Watson, C., Milner-Gulland, E. J., & Mourato, S. (2011). Direct Consumptive Use Value of Ecosystem Goods and Services in the Bale Mountains Eco-region, Ethiopia. *Journal of the Ethiopian Wildlife and Natural History Society*, Special Ed, 181–196.
Wherry, F. F. (2006). The nation-state, identity management , and indigenous crafts : Constructing markets and opportunities in Northwest Costa Rica. *Ethnic and Racial Studies*, 29(1), 124–152. doi:10.1080/01419870500352454
Yihune, M., Bekele, A., & Tefera, Z. (2008). Human – gelada baboon conflict in and around the Simien Mountains National Park , Ethiopia. *African Journal of Ecology,* 47, 276–282.
Zargham, H. (2007). Sustainable tourism development and handicrafts in the developing world. *Sustainable development and planning III*, 2, 1011–1017.
Zeleke, G. (2010). A Study on Mountain Externalities in Ethiopia.

ABOUT THE AUTHOR

Derek Lowstuter graduated with a B.S. degree in Natural Resource Management, with minors in Horticulture, Forestry, and History. He obtained his M.S. degree in Forest Sciences in collaboration with the Peace Corps Master's International Program. He is currently a doctoral student in Organizational Learning, Performance, and Change at Colorado State University. Derek works as an Agricultural and Food Systems Specialist at Colorado State University Extension. He has directed agricultural and natural resource management projects on four continents, but now calls Colorado Springs, CO, home with his wife Claire, their daughter, and a menagerie of animals and houseplants.

www.ingramcontent.com/pod-product-compliance
Lightning Source LLC
Chambersburg PA
CBHW042127160426
43198CB00021B/2935